Physical and Sexual Abuse of Children

Physical and Sexual Abuse of Children

Causes and Treatment

David R. Walters

Indiana University Press
Bloomington & London

National Standard Form—0023, Copyright © 1974, is
reproduced with the permission of the Children's
Division, The American Humane Association.

Published in Canada by Fitzhenry & Whiteside
Limited, Don Mills, Ontario

Manufactured in the United States of America

Library of Congress Cataloging in Publication Data
Walters, David R   1934-
Physical and sexual abuse of children.
Bibliography.
Includes index.
1. Cruelty to children—United States. I. Title.
[DNLM: 1. Child abuse. 2. Sex offenses. WA320 W235p]
HV741.W25   1975   364.1'5   75-1940
ISBN 0-253-34490-5
ISBN 0-253-34491-3 pbk.   1 2 3 4 5 79 78 77 76 75

For Bobbi

Contents

Preface

Several years ago a deputy chief of police of a midwestern city contacted me about an incident that was upsetting to his officers: An intoxicated mother and her boyfriend had casually tossed her eighteen-month-old child from a car window at 25 miles per hour. After I talked with the two adults in the county jail I was asked by the court if I would work with them if they were placed on probation. With some misgivings I agreed, and after that experience I began to specialize in treating abusive adults and their children.

As a practicing clinician in the field of child abuse, it is impossible for me at this point to minimize the impact of seeing children I know beaten, battered, or dead in the morgue. It is also impossible to theorize about a little girl I really cared about who was admitted to the hospital after a brutal sexual assault by her father. Conversely, it is difficult to minimize the influence of working with abusive parents who have been fired from their jobs, socially ostracized, and hounded daily as "monsters."

The physical and sexual abuse of children is not a very pleasant topic. Nearly every day news accounts dramatize the pain, suffering, and humiliation inflicted on children by parents and other adult caretakers. Rarely will the interested citizen read any further to learn what caused the abuse or how it was handled once reported, unless criminal prosecution results.

This book attempts to inform the reader about the overall problem of child abuse in America and to provide some understanding of adults who are labeled "abusive." It presents the human aspects of child abuse and how it can be treated by professionals, rather than a litany of horrors done to children. In fact, a deliberate effort has been made to avoid much of the emotionally charged aspects of abuse, simply because the abuse should be a beginning, rather than an end, to a treatment process whereby the children and adults are reintegrated into the community as nonabusive parents and non-abused children.

We will see that too often "treatment" of the abusive adult and abused child consists of systematic nontreatment through procedures and policies of the very agencies charged by law with offering services. More often than not, abusers are condemned, ignored but not forgotten, threatened with the loss of their children, and turned into social pariahs. They are labeled as "pathological" or "sociopathic" (or "psychopathic" if the professional has been out of school more than ten years) and are dealt with at arm's length. When and if treatment is offered, it is often based on an outmoded, unworkable model that suggests that abuse is the result of illness, that insight will cure the illness, and that the abuse will then cease.

From my own experience in working with a large number of offenders and their children I am convinced that the vast majority are not mentally ill or pathological. Consulting on over 2,000 abuse cases has reinforced rather than contradicted my basic views. It is the central thesis of this book that most abusive adults are simply repeating the patterns in which they were reared and that most do care about their children deeply, however misdirected and misguided their violence may be.

This book reflects my convictions that sexual abuse is completely different in aetiology than physical abuse, that current treatment or delivery systems are not working, and that abusers can and should be treated, as should their children. I also seriously question the current national effort in reporting cases of child abuse. The last chapter addresses itself to strategies for change, with suggestions as to how America might begin to approach this problem, which threatens to become a national disgrace.

Every author is probably asked, "What prompted you to write this book?" My motivation stemmed in part from my own experience in working with abusers but mainly from consulting around the country with those in public agencies charged with treating abuse. Most professionals are talented but have extremely high case loads. They are deeply troubled over the current system and are seeking alternatives. This book is an attempt to help them explore new ways of working with abuse situations. It is also written for others coming in contact with child abuse: physicians, police, lawyers, judges, nurses, teachers, social workers, and psychologists, as well as advanced undergraduate and graduate students.

With this audience in mind, I have made a deliberate effort to avoid the technical jargon of Ph.D.s in the social sciences. When it was necessary to discuss technical matters, I have tried to present the material in common-sense, everyday terms, using explanations or illustrations that everyone can understand. All references have been placed in the bibliography at the end of the book rather than at the end of each chapter.

Case material has been derived from my own practice in treating abusers and their children, and at times I have drawn upon materials provided me through consultation with agencies and other professionals. Names, dates, and places have been altered or eliminated to protect the anonymity of parents and children. No inferences should be drawn from any case or illustration to any abuse situation known to the reader.

Writing a book requires time and effort. One aspect, however, was pure fun and I would like to share that with the reader. In obtaining material related to our cultural heritage, I was given help by my "Research Assistants" Kimberly, Scott, Karen, John, Linda, and Stephanie. They provided me with their own favorite fairy tales, nursery rhymes, and "skip rope" ditties. To them, and numerous other children in Indiana, Florida, and Wisconsin, I am indebted and express my appreciation. They were also kind enough not to giggle too much as I clumsily skipped rope with them, and they reawakened joys long lost: catching bumblebees, lying on the grass watching the clouds, and playing "kick the can" in the evening.

Donald Martin of the University of Wisconsin-Oshkosh, William James of SUNY-Plattsburg, and J. Erroll Miller of Indiana University all gave me much-needed moral support at different times in completing this book. Victor Streib—attorney, friend, and colleague at Indiana University—gave me many hours of his time in legal advice, intellectual "cross-examination," and encouragement. To each of them, and many others, I am indebted and express my thanks.

Personally and professionally, appreciation is also expressed to the many "abusive" parents it has been my privilege to know and treat. They have made this book possible by educating me, and they have made me a better parent. In helping me to understand their humanity, they have assisted me in better understanding my own.

Physical and Sexual Abuse of Children

CHAPTER ONE

Nature and Extent of Child Abuse

Child abuse is pandemic in the United States. Few children grow to adulthood and escape the parental hand raised in anger. More often than not an object such as a hairbrush, switch, belt, or ironing cord is used to inflict pain on the child. In some instances children suffer a whip, fan belt, clothesline, steam, fire, cigarette burns, or a blowtorch. Some spend long hours tied to a bed, in basements or attics, or locked out of the house. Some are not fed. Relatively few die, however, yet most who do are young, very young. Few parents who abuse their children are reported to the authorities, and most of those who are reported deny the abuse. Few are prosecuted and few are treated by professionals.

These observations may at first glance appear startling, puzzling, or confusing to the layperson. Surely if a child is maltreated or abused in America, it would logically follow that the child should receive the necessary medical and psychological treatment and that the adult abuser would be processed through either the criminal justice or the mental health delivery system. Commonly, persons not familiar with child abuse assume that the children desire to be removed permanently from the presence of the parents or adults abusing them and that "no one in his right mind" would ever harm a child. Consequently, it also follows that the abusive adult should receive some attention from society. Depending on the orientation of the observer, the interested citizen might call for punishment of the

3

abuser or for some sort of "treatment." Often, both are desired, such as "treating" the abuser in prison—an impossibility if there ever was one.

Contrary to public opinion, most children who are abused do not feel victimized. They frequently feel worse about bringing adverse attention to the parents who have abused them than they do about being abused. Medical personnel know only too well that most abused children try to fabricate excuses for their adult abusers' behavior and often feel guilty because they require medical treatment. And, rather than being contrite over abuse incidents, most adults who abuse their children are openly hostile over what they feel is unwarranted interference with their parental right to correct their children.

It is the thesis of this book that the physical and sexual abuse of children is usually not inflicted by mentally ill or pathological parents. Rather, it is the logical outgrowth of our cultural heritage and predilection toward violence. In order to understand the total problem, we will first examine what little we know about the problem, discuss the cultural facets that generate and encourage the abuse of children, and examine different types of abusers and how they might be treated. We will also view common social-agency practices and attitudes to understand why virtually nothing is being done about the problem. Finally, we will discuss treatment, public policy, and legislative strategies that may alleviate it. It is hoped that the reader will obtain a better understanding of the problem and perhaps of the children and adults involved in this drama of harm, which is played out each and every day in the United States. Consider the following two cases:

Jane, age 4, was left with her mother's boyfriend. He wanted to marry Jane's mother but did not want the responsibility of the little girl. He beat Jane repeatedly, and the child continually asked her mother, neighbors, and relatives, "Is 'Daddy' going to kill me?" Jane was never admitted to the hospital, but was taken directly to the morgue. She was beaten to death with fists and an iron rod, and had lacerations all over her body. It seemed that only one thing remained untouched and unharmed, the small cross on a gold chain around her neck, given to her by the man who killed her. Charged with murder, he pleaded innocent. On a negotiated plea of guilty to a reduced charge of manslaughter, he received a sentence in the state penitentiary of one to three years.

Neighbors had reported Jonah's mother several times for unmercifully beating him. One evening she beat him with a broomstick for failing to clean up his room, the living room, and the kitchen. After knocking him unconscious, she put him on the back porch and left to go "partying" at 9 P.M. At midnight, hearing moans, neighbors investigated and found Jonah on the back porch, alone and uncovered in 30° weather. He was rushed to the hospital but expired in two hours. Apparently he had regained consciousness at one point and reentered the house, for the police found a plaintive note on the kitchen table:

> Mom:
> I'm sorry for not cleaning up. I
> love you.
>
> Jonah

It seems that he was fearful of his mother's wrath when she returned home and had returned to the back porch. The mother was charged with murder.

Several questions come to mind: How many Janes and Jonahs are there in this country each year? Why did these events occur? Why didn't someone do something after both children were known to be in danger? Were the adults mentally ill? Were the dispositions "proper"? Can the adults be treated? Can such incidents be prevented?

Today and tonight, in thousands of American homes, children will be "spanked" or "switched" for various kinds of misbehavior by well-meaning and loving parents. Are we dealing with differences in degree or kind when we think of these parents as opposed to Jane's and Jonah's aggressors?

Solution Counseling

Physical

The actual number of abused children in the United States each year is unknown. As we will see later, there are many reasons for the lack of reliable statistics, among them differences in definition, failure to report instances of abuse, and immunity from reporting if the abusers are of sufficient income, social status, or class to be referred to private practitioners rather than to public agencies. Almost all reported, known child abuse cases have this in common: They are severe or gross enough that several sources agree that abuse has occurred. DeFrancis of the American Humane Association (Stoenner, 1973) estimated 25,000 cases per year. Zalba (1966) estimated 30,000 to 37,500. Other estimates have ranged from 250,000 up. If one were to define abuse simply as an adult's striking a child in anger, the figure would be astronomical.

Definitional and reporting problems aside, we do know certain facts about the overall problem and results of abuse. The very term "child abuse" implies that the victims are young or are at least under age. Most children who are abused are not enrolled in school or found on the playing fields of high schools. The vast majority are too young to enter school, and many are infants. While differences exist among researchers as to where the preponderance of cases is found, all who have studied the problem—including Terr and Watson (1968), Paulson and Blake (1969), Heins (1969), Fontana (1971a), Michael (1970), Ebbin, Gollub, Stein, and Wilson (1969), and Zuckerman et al. (1972)—have observed that many more cases involve infants and young children than older children.

If children live until they are able to crawl, their chances of physical survival increase, and if they live until they can walk or run, their chances increase dramatically. This does not mean that they will not bear scars, for many will. Sometimes the injuries are unseen, and multiple fractures go unnoticed unless for some reason X-rays are taken. As a result of being abused by adults, some children will be permanently damaged. Elmer and Gregg (1967) have noted the presence of mental retardation, central nervous system damage, and speech defects. Brain damage, emotional problems, and failure to grow also have been observed by Wright (1970), Kempe and Helfer (1972), and Evans, Reinhart, and Succop (1972).

This pattern of child rearing is not accidental, and the infliction of physical pain on children is purposive. It is one of the core components in American child-rearing philosophy. The infliction of pain becomes "abusive" only when the laws, community, neighborhood, agencies, and usually a publicly employed social worker make the assessment that the parent has "gone too far" or raised his or her hand once too often with too much vigor.

Many female children are approached for sexual gratification by adult males, and many male children are approached by adult male homosexuals. Contrary to public belief, sexual exploiters and abusers of children are not strangers, but in the vast majority of instances are well known to the children and are related to them through kinship or marriage. Often, the abuser is the child's natural father or stepfather, uncle, brother-in-law, or other relative.

Who are these children? If we are talking about physical violence, they are most of the children in this country. And if we are speaking of sexual abuse, there are many more cases than even the most pessimistic professional would estimate. The children are of all races and religions; their parents are affluent and poor, educated and uneducated; they live in urban centers and rural settings. Some of the children are of high intelligence, some are normal, and some are retarded. Some are physically handicapped, but most are not. Abuse does not only occur in homes. Many children who do not face abuse at home may be subjected to punishment, striking, slapping, "whippings," and much worse in schools, foster homes, day care centers, detention homes, or other public and private institutions.

If a child is severely abused, or harmed to the point of requiring medical attention, the physical abuser (usually the parent) will be reported to the authorities but rarely will he or she be prosecuted for repeated assaults on the child. If prosecuted, the abuser need not fear jail, for it is unlikely that a conviction will be brought by a jury composed of parents who have also subjected their children to violence. Instead, society will try to "treat" the unwilling adult abuser and will fail in this endeavor. If the professional charged with treating the abuser is persistent and becomes a "nuisance" to the abuser, there are still several avenues open. One tactic, which is not infrequently used, is simply to "move over the county line," out of the professional's jurisdiction. Another is to leave the state, for no one will know of the abuser elsewhere.

In most instances, the abused child will mature, grow to adulthood, in turn become a parent, and perpetuate the use of force on children. This has been the story of child abuse in America.

CHAPTER TWO

Cultural Causes and History

The physical and sexual abuse of children does not occur in a cultural vacuum. Rather, America has a long history of treating children as inferiors, as little more than chattel to be done with as the adult caretaker wishes.

The status of children in present-day America has its roots in history, specifically in the Bible. For generations, we have been a people strongly influenced by the Bible. We have tried to pattern our lives after its teachings, and to a large degree this book has influenced our interpersonal relationships, our handling of children, and the status of children in our society. Out of our Judeo-Christian heritage came laws that formalized the biblical status, roles, and relationships, and today attorneys are still struggling with legal problems connected with the abuse of children.

There are some who believe that the Industrial Revolution and the increase in technology are the primary causes of child abuse. This is difficult to support in view of other, nonindustrial and nontechnological cultures that also permit the abuse of children. Nevertheless, for exactly the same reason that abuse was permitted, i.e., because of our Judeo-Christian heritage, so has an awareness developed over the raw exploitation of children, for biblically speaking, no one—adult or child—should be subjected to torture and subsequent death who abides by and subscribes to the tenets articulated in the Bible.

The status of children is further reinforced by fairy tales, nursery rhymes, and other cultural influences that clarify the child's position and lack of power in interpersonal relationships. From these factors, a cultural base for the occurrence of child abuse rises.

The Bible

Part of the difficulty in understanding harsh treatment of children in the Bible rests with the very definition of children. In some instances the "children" are obviously adults, even grandparents, as in such references as "children of God," "children of Israel," "son of man," and "daughter of Jerusalem." In spite of this vagueness, we do know of many instances in which children were made to suffer death, sometimes on a quite impersonal basis. In 1 Samuel 15 we find the injunction to "slay both man and woman, child and suckling . . ." in order to punish Amalec. We also find the same command for the murder of Assyrians, Ammonites, Moabites, Edomites, Canaanites, and others.

Most religious people in America celebrate the Feast of Passover, as explained in Exodus:

> For I will pass through the land of Egypt this night, and smite all the firstborn in the land of Egypt, both man and beast, and against all the Gods of Egypt I will execute: I am the Lord. And the Blood (on the lintel of the houses of the faithful) shall be to you for a token upon the houses where you are: and when I see the blood, I will pass over you, and the plague shall not be upon you to destroy you, when I smite the land of Egypt. [Exodus 12: 12, 13]

The sacrifice of children is not unknown either. The book of Judges tells of Jephthah's victory over the Ammonites. Before the battle, Jephthah promises that if his forces win, he will sacrifice the first person who meets him upon his return. Victorious, he is greeted by his only daughter, who is sacrificed. In the rebuilding of the city of Jericho, Hiel, the Bethelite, sacrificed his firstborn, Abiram, in the foundation and his youngest son, Segub, beneath the gates.

In the Old Testament cannibalism of children is to be found. For example, the children of Israel are told that if they do not follow the commandments, "Then I will walk contrary unto you also in fury; and I, even I, will chastise you seven times for your sins. And ye shall eat the flesh of your sons, and the flesh of your daughters shall ye eat" (Leviticus 26: 28, 29). In another instance, when the king of Israel was passing through Samaria during a famine he was approached by a mother who had boiled and eaten her child one day, with the understanding that another mother would boil her child the following day (2 Kings 6).

Children are enjoined to honor and obey parents and older persons. Those who do not will suffer grievous consequences. In 2 Kings 2, as Elisha was going to Bethel, "there came forth little children out of the city, and mocked him. . . ." Elisha cursed them in the name of the Lord, and immediately "two she bears" came out of the woods and tore forty and two children. In Deuteronomy we are told that if parents take a rebellious son to the elders of the city and tell them, "This our son is stubborn and rebellious, he will not obey our voice; he is a glutton and a drunkard," the men of the city will stone him to death.

Parents are given instructions as to how to raise children. One of the biblical "justifications" that has resulted in much abuse is Proverbs. This book tells us, "He that spareth the rod hateth his son: but he that loveth him chasteneth him betimes," and "Chasten thy son while there is hope, and let not thy soul spare for his crying." Closely following these come other suggestions or orders to "Train up a child . . . ," along with the assurance, "Withhold not correction from the child; for if thou beatest him with the rod, he shall not die. Thou shall beat him with a rod, and shalt deliver his soul from Hell." These and many other Old Testament injunctions support parental harm to children.

In the area of sexual abuse, incest and incest taboo are discussed a great deal in the Old Testament. In Genesis, Lot's two daughters get him intoxicated and seduce him. Both become pregnant as a result. This drama of father and daughter having sexual relations has been repeated time and again. From the story of Lot and his daughters, we inherit the cultural belief that, in many instances, the daughter seduces the father and that the father is intoxicated and the "innocent victim" of the seduction. This stigma and the results of incest are found in the offspring of the incestuous liaison: from those two nights came Moab, father of the Moabites, and Benammi, father of the children of Ammon. The curse of God was put on bastards, "who shall not enter into the congregation of the Lord," and because Moab and Benammi were conceived in a father-daughter union we are told also in Deuteronomy that, "An Ammonite or Moabite shall not enter the congregation of the Lord; even to their tenth generation shall they not enter into the congregation of the Lord for ever."

In all, the Old Testament laid the foundation for many of the beliefs we hold today in the realms of child rearing, the status of children, and sexual relations. And these injunctions, beliefs, and actions are transmitted daily and on Sunday, in many churches throughout America. Those who object to the view that the Bible sanctions this behavior state that the citations are taken out of context and that the meanings of the passages differ; they can also cite passages in which parents are admonished to care for their children. Nevertheless, in their totality, the biblical injunctions do constitute the grounds on which many punish and, indeed, abuse children.

Unfortunately, while clerics differ in interpretation, parents in the last analysis become their own doctors of divinity and select those passages meaningful to them, from which have arisen harsh, swift, and punitive manners of dealing with children. In support of these practices, public schools, local and state child-caring institutions, and private, religiously based schools and institutions have many times found justification for horrors perpetrated on children.

Literary Influences

As part of the developmental and maturational process, children of each culture are exposed to fairy tales, nursery rhymes, and lore which prepare them for life. Part of the function of this literature is to transmit role expectations and the expected interrelationships among people. Our culture is no different from any other insofar as this process is concerned. Mothers croon to babies and sing songs. Children sing, skip rope to ditties handed down for generations, and listen to stories that entertain them and educate them to our culture. Folk songs and folk tales have been handed down and modified for hundreds of years. Many of these stories were European in origin and were brought to the new land by immigrants and assimilated into our culture.

Many rhymes, songs, and stories contain varying degrees of violence done to children and to adults for failing to abide by the wishes of others. Children are enjoined to obey their parents lest disaster befall them. They are also told repeatedly how helpless they are against the elements, the environment, strangers, and the forces of evil.

For hundreds of years children have been exposed to the following rhyme, which is melodic but nevertheless carries the message of helplessness:

> Rock-a-bye, baby, on the treetop,
> When the wind blows, the cradle will rock;
> When the bough breaks, the cradle will fall,
> And down will come baby, cradle and all.

Little Polly Flinders and Tom, the Piper's Son, illustrate the consequences of self-indulgence:

> Little Polly Flinders
> Sat among the cinders
> Warming her pretty little toes.
> Her mother came and caught her
> And whipped her little daughter
> For spoiling her nice new clothes.

> Tom, Tom, the piper's son,
> Stole a pig, and away he run.
> The pig was eat, and Tom was beat,
> And Tom went roaring down the street.

Sometimes, of course, children suffer because an adult is being overwhelmed:

There was an old woman who lived in a shoe,
She had so many children she didn't know what to do;
She gave them some broth without any bread,
And whipped them all soundly and sent them to bed.

Children are in part acclimated to the expectations of school by their exposure to Dr. Faustus—who was a good man:

Doctor Faustus was a good man,
He whipped his scholars now and then;
When he whipped them he made them dance
Out of England into France,
Out of France into Spain
And then he whipped them back again!

Children who are tattletales or thieves are given the message:

Charley, Charley,
Stole the barley
Out of the baker's shop.
The baker came out
And gave him a clout,
Which made poor Charley hop.

Rather common jump rope rhymes also convey the message to children, as in the following:

Into the cistern little Willie
Pushed his little sister Lilly
Mother couldn't find her daughter
Now we sterilize our water.

Fudge, Fudge call the judge
Mama has a newborn baby
It isn't a boy
It isn't a girl
It's just an ordinary baby.
Wrap it up in tissue paper
Throw it down the elevator

First floor, miss
Second floor, miss
Third floor, miss
Fourth . . . [continued until the jumper misses].

Down by the ocean, down by the sea,
Johnny broke a milk bottle
And blamed it on me
I told Ma, Ma told Pa,
Johnny got a spanking, Ha, Ha, Ha.
How many spankings did he get?
[Count until the jumper misses.]

Stories also convey certain cultural messages. Aesop's *Fables* tell children of the pitfalls of life that await them and of the retribution for behavior not deemed appropriate by society. The shepherd boy who cried "Wolf" when there was none points up the consequences of lying. Some other dangers of misbehavior are recounted in the tales of "The Wolf and the Goat," "The Cat and the Mice," "The Hen and the Fox," "The Country Mouse and the Town Mouse," and "The Fox and the Crow."

In the familiar story of "Jack and the Beanstalk" some have difficulty remembering how the beanstalk came about, but all children remember the rhyme of the ogre.

Fee-fi-fo-fum,
I smell the blood of an Englishman.
Be he alive, or be he dead,
I'll grind his bones to make my bread.

All children know of the perils of wandering off when they should not and of the dangers that might befall them, particularly in strange places such as the forest. Little Red Ridinghood, who disobeyed her mother by tarrying along the way on her humanitarian errand of taking cake and a bottle of wine to her grandmother, was swallowed by a wolf. Fortunately, a huntsman who heard the wolf snoring had the thought that perhaps the wolf had swallowed the

aged grandmother and cut it open. Lo, and behold! It was Little
Red Ridinghood *and* her grandmother!

Another little girl, Goldilocks, disobeyed her mother, and because she "was not at all a well brought up little girl" she entered the
house of the three bears, ate their porridge, sat in their chairs, and
lay in their beds. "Naughty Goldilocks jumped out the window, and
whether she broke her neck in the fall, or ran in the wood and was
lost there, or found her way out of the wood and got whipped for
being a bad girl and playing truant, no one can say" (Martignoni,
1955).

These stories, and literally hundreds more, represent the indoc-
trination we give children. Adults usually say that they heard these
stories when they were children and were not scared by them. That
may be true for children whose parents are sensitive, but many
parents are not and try to frighten their children, telling them that
what happened to the bad children in the stories will befall them if
they persist in their wayward behavior. Even this message need not
be directly conveyed by the adults, for the stories tell it well.

Children are unable to differentiate between fact and fancy,
between the real and the unreal. Just consider the effect of imagination when a child feels and honestly believes that an animal—usually
ferocious—is lurking under the bed, just waiting for dark so it can
harm the child. Students of children's literature are often not so
surprised by the content of the tales, having heard them as children,
as by the illustrations that accompany them. In books prepared and
published for children, the child is usually depicted as being very
small, and the ogre, or whatever other threat exists, is oversized in
relation to the child. So are adult figures, with "mean" adults being
two, three, or four times the size of the child.

Legal History

Children's roles and legal status are the direct result of the
patriarchal Judeo-Christian heritage given to us by the Bible. Like
women, children were considered to have less status than adult
men. In theory, both benefited from their support and protection

against external threat and pressure. In return, the father or other male assumed dominance within the household and could, with impunity in many instances, kill his wife and/or children without admonishment. This was particularly true in the families of rulers or royalty, among whom the paternal right of killing was exercised frequently.

Paternal control was complete, and the distinction of parental control did not evolve until the publication in A.D. 726 of *Ecloga,* which was issued in the name of Leo III and Constantine V. Guardianship was not concerned with the rights or possessions of children either. Earlier and in the common law, it conferred a valuable right upon the guardian—that of the child's labor.

For thousands of years then, the lot of children was harsh and cruel. They were "fair game" in the labor market, and it was not until the 1800s that the difference between children and adults was recognized in England. In 1802 the practice of apprenticing children to cotton mill owners was theoretically curtailed, by limiting children to twelve hours of labor in the mills per day. Unfortunately, this law had no enforcement provision and was disregarded. The Factory Act, passed in 1833 during the Grey cabinet of England, prohibited child labor under the age of 9, and restricted children under 14 to forty-eight hours of work per week. Under the Benthamite doctrine, the 1834 law regulating poorhouses intentionally created exceedingly harsh conditions in order to insure that the fewest number of persons would go on relief. Families suffered, and from *Oliver Twist* we learn that children were not exempted.

Many of the English laws, like all laws and court decisions, were more honored in the breach rather than in the observance. As late as 1842 a Royal Commission reported children as young as 5 and 6 of both sexes working sixteen hours a day in the coal mines. As a result, in the same year, an act was passed—against the wishes of the House of Lords—prohibiting all females and boys under 10 from working in the mines.

Under the law, children under the age of 7 have traditionally been thought of as being incapable of harboring criminal intent and were largely exempted from criminal penalties. Between the ages of 7 and 14, they were presumed to be innocent of criminal intent; however, prosecutors could and did offer arguments to the contrary. History records instances in England as late as the early 1800s of a girl of 7 who was publicly hanged, a child of 13 hanged for stealing a spoon, and a boy of 9 sentenced to death for stealing an item worth tuppence from a printer.

Humaneness expressed itself in a great wave in the 1800s in the Western world. The year 1824 saw the founding of the National Society for the Prevention of Cruelty to Animals (in England) and the Royal Scottish Society for the Prevention of Cruelty to Animals. Children were not to receive similar protection until a half-century later, probably because animals were "dumb" and children were not. The same spirit expressed itself in America. In 1874 in New York, the now-famous case of Mary Ellen arose. Laws preventing cruelty to animals were invoked to rescue the child, who had been abused by her foster mother. Finally, largely in the twentieth century, child protection laws came into being, and child abuse has theoretically been prohibited.

Thus we must conclude that children have been an expendable commodity for thousands of years—exploited, worked to death, slain, and tortured by some parents, guardians, and employers. Only very recently have children been offered any protection. And because of this history, we now find that laws in the field of child abuse are, at best, embryonic. When law evolves, it is based on prior law and decisions, and, for this reason, two thousand years of absolute parental rights will not fade away overnight. In fact, even in constructing the most enlightened law protecting children, the rights of the parents and adult caretakers will take precedence over the children's lives for years to come.

Because the laws are not enforceable against parents, children are often killed with impunity, denied medical treatment and even allowed to die to "prove" their parents' faith, and are beaten, maimed and tortured. Fathers are in fact allowed to treat their children as chattel, to have sexual relations with their daughters, and have only to fear the censure of the community. They need not fear prosecution and imprisonment, as statistics in America show us.

In the light of our cultural history, it is very understandable that our society is abusive. This country was founded by people seeking religious freedom, and the Bible was and is studied carefully in many American homes. As we have seen, parents may do anything they wish to children to "save their souls." The law reflects that heritage, and even the common songs, rhymes, and tales of children reiterate their helplessness and the dire consequences of incurring the wrath of an adult.

CHAPTER THREE

Recent Views of Child Abuse

Research in the field of child abuse is relatively recent and largely came about through the discovery of the "battered child syndrome." This led to an interest in the severely abused child, medical management of the injuries, identification of the parent or adult caretaker likely to abuse a child, and subsequent treatment of the adult so that the severe abuse would not recur.

The purely medical aspects of child abuse were pioneered in an article published in 1946 in the *American Journal of Roentgenology* by Dr. John Caffey, who drew attention to unexplained fractures in various stages of healing in the long bones in infants. Later, Caffey (1957) concluded that these injuries might have been caused by parents who intentionally harmed their children, although he did not suggest which parents or under what conditions the abuse might have occurred. After the initial spate of medical literature, people in many fields became interested in child abuse, and several hundred articles and books have been addressed in whole or in part to this very perplexing problem.

Causes of Abuse

In the literature the search for the causes of abuse seems endless. Major trends are seen, but the determination of causative forces more often than not reflects the discipline and training of the author or the orientation of the agency he or she represents. Many writers see multiple causes, which are difficult to research because it is nearly impossible to hold certain variables constant in order to obtain any idea of the "load factor" of each cause.

Poverty is given much stress in Gil's (1973) orientation and view of the problem. Others who share Gil's view that economic pressures or adversity of the parents cause or contribute to child abuse are Brown and Daniels (1968), Weston (1968), Fontana (1971b), Toussaint (1971), Sattin and Miller (1971), and Zuckerman et al. (1972). Some believe that many impoverished families are of a low socioeconomic class, and low class status is given weight as a factor by Elmer (1967), Elmer and Gregg (1967), and Strauss and Wolf (1969).

The excessive use of alcohol and the presence of alcoholism in the home are cited and given emphasis by Jeffress (1967), Pospisil-Zavrski and Turcin (1968), Fontana (1971a, 1971b), Pawlikowski (1972), and Wertham (1972).

—— Neglect by parents or caretakers in and of itself (i.e., without too much emphasis on why the neglect occurred) is considered important in the aetiology of child abuse by Nau and Cabanis (1966), Rose, Hirschenfang, and Benton (1967), and Weston (1968).

There seems to be a question whether family stress results in the abuse of children. It arises because after the discovery and reporting of abuse, the family is placed in a stressful situation; sometimes the loss of children, spouse, home, or job is threatened. Some feel that stress in the family, in and of itself, preceded the abusive act.

Those giving weight to family disruption, breakdown, and stress are Elmer (1966, 1967), Brown and Daniels (1968), Bennie and Sclare (1969), Biermann (1969), Terr (1970), Silver, Dublin, and Lourie (1971), Fontana (1971b), Havens (1972), and James (1972).

Other factors are mental retardation in the parents, noted by Holter and Friedman (1968) and Weston (1968); organicity, by Birrell and Birrell (1968); "organic neural overload," by Baron, Bejar, Rafael, and Sheaff (1970); and "organic inferiority," by Curtis (1963).

By far the greatest emphasis in the literature is on the belief that the physical abuse of children is the result of severe emotional pressures on one or both parents or of neurosis or psychosis. This, of course, is the view of many psychiatrists and mental health professionals who are trained to see internal dysfunction in the individual as being causative of an outward symptom. Writers who have stressed psychosis and individual pathology in the abuser are represented in part by Jeffress (1967), Holter and Friedman (1968), Birrell and Birrell (1968), Pospisil-Zavrski and Turcin (1968), Steele (1968), Asch (1968), Flynn (1970), Laury (1970), Wright (1970), Pickel, Anderson, and Holiday (1970), Richette (1969), Pavenstedt and Bernard (1971), Fontana (1971b), D'Ambrosio (1970), Wertham (1972), and Spinetta and Rigler (1972).

The issues become more confusing when one looks at the traits of the abusers. In nearly all instances, when such descriptions are given, they are viewed as pathological and carry unsavory and undesirable connotations. Many, as we noted, are viewed as psychotic. Some of the labels that have been applied are "schizoid psychopaths" (Fleming, 1967), "psychopath and aggressive brute" (Birrell and Birrell, 1968), and "oligophrenic, sadistic and psychopathic" (Laury, 1970).

Currently there are three widely accepted views of the causes of child abuse. Bakan (1971) makes a very good argument that our entire cultural heritage leads us to permit the abuse of children. He takes the position that our Judeo-Christian tradition coupled with our predilection for violence make abuse a natural, rather than unnatural, outcome. He proposes as a solution the internalization of parts of the *Universal Declaration of Human Rights,* adopted by the United Nations in 1949: Article 5, which prohibits torture, cruel, inhuman, or degrading treatment or punishment; and Article 25, which guarantees adequate health, food, clothing, medical care, security, and a standard of living, along with preferential treatment of mothers and children.

Somewhat related to Bakan's stand is that taken by Gil in his book, *Violence Against Children* (1973). In this work, which consisted of a nationwide survey of reported child abuse in America, Gil posited that the cause (and ultimate solution) to the problem was to be found in poverty conditions: lack of income, health care,

and social services; run-down neighborhoods; and inadequate housing, education, and cultural and recreational facilities, all of which
contributed to the development of deviant behavior or pathology,
which resulted in child abuse. Gil's finding that poverty seemed a
determinant is quite understandable. His data were obtained from
agencies that had a clientele of poor people. Abusers who had
money, attorneys, social status, prestige, and a high reputation in
the community were usually referred to private practitioners (which
means their cases were not reported to a public agency for statistical
purposes).

The third suggested cause of child abuse might be described as
the pathological view, which assumes that the parent or adult abuser
is "sick" or has something psychiatrically or psychologically
"wrong." This opinion is widely held by many mental health professionals and some of the public. It holds that, to greater or lesser
degrees, the abusers of America are confused and employ abusive
measures as a result of internal pathology.

Leontine Young, in *Wednesday's Children* (1964), employed
a theory of multiple causation, or a combination of factors that
lead to abuse. Among them were the abuse that parents themselves
suffered as children, institutionalization, "being different from other
members of the family," an unpleasant childhood, neglect, and possible organic differences.

Another view is offered in the present book: Child abuse in
most instances is a learned behavior. It is a type of child rearing
that can be predicted, treated, and, in the last analysis, prevented if
society is committed to doing something about the problem. Most
abusive parents are not mentally ill, and there are many types of
physical abuse, not just one.

Current schools of thought consider child abuse not as a problem in itself but as another symptom of an evil, sick, or negative
aspect of society. Poverty, alcohol, family stress, neglect, social class,
individual pathology, and related "causes" have all been used at one
time or another to explain crime, mental illness, mental retardation,
juvenile delinquency, and a host of other problems.

C. Henry Kempe, one of the original researchers and pioneers in the field of child abuse, has articulated a view that questions the positions taken by many other researchers—a view that merits close examination, for it has great bearing on treatment efforts in the field. In 1971 Kempe took issue with stereotypic notions about the cause of abuse and the characteristics of abusers, stating that 90 percent of the abusing parents appeared to have no serious problems. In 1972, along with others, he repeated this view. If Kempe's assumptions and views are correct, serious questions must be raised about treating child abuse, particularly physical abuse. The traditional mental health/social work axis then must also be questioned, as it would be applicable in the treatment of only 10 percent of the cases. If Kempe is correct, and there is increasing support for his position, new treatment models must be developed separate and apart from the pathological model. In physical abuse there no longer seems to be any doubt that the vast majority of abusers can be helped through alternative programs and strategies.

Problems in Defining Abuse

As noted earlier, no one can estimate with any degree of accuracy the frequency or the extent of physical and sexual abuse of children in America. Any estimate, whether it be 50,000 or 500,000 cases per year must be suspect for several reasons: Physical violence in child raising is not only permitted but encouraged; child abuse is often defined on the basis of injury; and definitions vary. To illustrate the problems of defining abuse we might examine the following:

Johnny is struck by his father for misbehavior. His hand strikes the boy's face, leaving temporary imprints of his hand, which eventually fade. Johnny cries.

Johnny is struck by his father for misbehavior. His hand is directed to the boy's face, but Johnny turns his head. The blow hits Johnny's ear, rupturing the eardrum. Johnny is off balance and strikes his head against the wall. Johnny is unconscious and is taken to the hospital, where it is found that his skull is fractured.

In the first instance, normal and acceptable American child-rearing practices are at work, while the second would be classified as "abuse" on the basis of Johnny's injuries. In the former case we have a good father concerned over his child's misbehavior; when the latter is discovered and reported, we would look for mental illness or call the father a brute.

Or, we might consider three additional situations:

Mrs. A., a welfare client, enters a tavern at 11 P.M., leaving her three children asleep in the car. She is reported to the police, and Mrs. A. is charged with neglect.

Mrs. A., a welfare client, enters a tavern at 11 P.M., leaving her three children asleep in the car. The temperature is —20°, and the police find the children nearly frozen. Mrs. A. is charged with abuse.

Mrs. N., wife of an up-and-coming bank employee, leaves her son in the car in the parking lot of a suburban shopping center for "a few minutes." The car windows are rolled up, and the inside temperature reaches 120°. On her return, Mrs. N. finds the boy unconscious and rushes him to a hospital. The child quickly recovers. Mrs. N is "in shock" and is comforted by her husband and sedated by her physician. No charges are filed.

Thus, we see that not only can the child's movement and proximity to a wall result in the label of abuse, as with Johnny, but also social status, environmental factors, the method of reporting to authorities, parental behavior, and the rapidity with which medical treatment is given all may be determinants in whether an abuse complaint is filed.

Cultural differences among geographical areas in the United States also account for differences in interpretation, definition, and reporting of abuse, and, in turn, they skew the statistics. In some areas, use of the "hickory stick," "switch," and other instruments used to inflict pain on children are thoroughly assimilated into the subculture and folklore. In others, it is not. Thus, what may be considered abuse in the rural area of one state may not be in the city, and vice-versa. Further, what may be held to be abusive in the South may not necessarily be so in the East or the Midwest, and that which is abusive in the Southwest may not necessarily be so elsewhere. The literature in the area of sexual abuse of children is sparse, insofar as it is related to the general topic of abuse. There are a number of anthropological studies on the matter of incest that disprove the myth that a universal, cross-cultural taboo exists. Reports of father-daughter relations in our own and other cultures are not uncommon, but Reichal-Dolmatoff (1951) has written a most interesting account of the behavior of mothers and sons among the Kogi of Colombia, who represent the exception to the incest rules. In America, it is quite rare that mother-son relationships come to the attention of reporting agencies.

It is even more difficult to define sexual abuse than physical. Consider the following cases:

Father walks around nude in the house most of the time and encourages his two teen-age girls to do so. They object; he insists. They reluctantly comply.

Father walks around nude in the house and encourages his two teen-age daughters to do so. They comply. Father makes remarks about their breasts. A neighbor observes this and reports the situation.

Father walks around nude, encourages his two teen-age daughters to do so, and they comply. He "wrestles" on the bed with one while nude, has an erection, and sexual relations result.

The first two instances generally would not be considered sexually abusive. The father might be chastised for lack of judgment in the second, but probably would not be in the first. In the third, he would be considered by the lay public as "crazy" or a "sex maniac." Professionals would look for "pathology."

Child abuse then, is not a clear-cut case of cause and effect. In part, it is due to situational factors: the actions and behaviors of the abuser and the abusee; their motivations; social status; to whom, how, and under what circumstances the event is reported; and the cultural setting in which the actions occurred.

The definition of abuse is therefore a difficult task. Some writers have not defined it, assuming that all who are interested in the topic have a commonality of understanding. Others have defined physical abuse in vague dimensions, but as behavior not within the experience of middle-class citizens. Generally, under the law and in the minds of professionals and public alike, child abuse is something that is harmful to a child, is deemed "excessive," and is more than the observer or commentator would employ in correcting a child. With the current situation and lack of definition, we rarely know if we are all talking about the same phenomenon because of our lack of commitment to children. However, if we can obtain any consensus on philosophical issues, the problem of definition will be much simpler. Definition is extremely important, for from it flows research, understanding of the issues, and development of effective treatment programs.

Some definitions are so broad as to encompass nearly every type of behavior. The bulk of abuse cases are variously characterized as physical, moral, emotional, medical, community, and educational "neglect." Some have spoken of "religious neglect," implying that children who are unfortunate enough to have parents who are agnostics or atheists or who do not expose them to Christian ideology are abused.

"Child abuse" is basically a negative judgment about the parental ability or behavior of another. Generally, the person who is abusing is assumed to be chronologically older than the person abused. Usually, the abuser is an adult. Within this context, physical abuse can be defined as follows:

> Physical abuse of a child is action taken by a parent or adult caretaker that results in physical harm or injury to the child or failure to act on a child's behalf wherein death of the child will result from continued inaction or neglect.

The definition of physical abuse does not address itself to the question of intent, which may be germane to the law but is meaningless in the social sciences in this particular area. In one instance of physical abuse we may find deliberation and premeditation by an adult, and, in another, the adult may simply lash out at a child and cause harm. Yet we cannot say that the child's pain or injury is less in the latter than in the former. The focus of the definition, then, is not on the adult, but on the child and the effect of the adult's behavior, regardless of intent.

The second part of the definition of physical abuse addresses itself to the problem of neglect, or failure to act on a child's behalf. The terms *neglect* and *abuse* are not interchangeable. Although they share the same negative judgment about rearing children and perhaps the capacity for being a parent, they are substantively different. The first implies failure to act, the second an inaction deemed harmful and deliberate. The concept of "neglect" also implies a failure to act in a manner which is determined to be appropriate by the observer who defines the act. As such it is a value judgment and becomes another arsenal in the weapon of professionals who are irritated by their clients' or patients' behavior.

Most agencies are staffed by white, middle-class persons who cannot or will not accept differing life styles. For this reason and others, the second part of our definition is restricted to death of the child as a result of continued neglect or inaction. This decision can and should be based on information from physicians, public health nurses, and others representing the medical profession.

Within the context of this definition, the parent whose child goes to school dirty or is not given adequate meals may be deficient as a parent but should not be defined as abusive. Further, the definition can and should be extended to cover the child living in a house that lacks plumbing or has outhouses draining into play areas and gardens and to the city child whose life is threatened by rats and vermin. Too often, agencies have decried children's dirty faces and dirty clothes but have failed to provide sanitary facilities or to prohibit the use of grossly substandard housing for fear of alienating slumlords or city housing agencies.

Restricting the definition of neglect should in no way minimize the seriousness of its effects. Certainly the child who appears at school dirty or with inadequate clothing deserves the attention, concern, and aid of society. Without a doubt, the child's self-image is affected adversely, and his or her ability to function is limited as a result of these parental practices or parental inaction. While the parents may need assistance and/or correction, they should not be defined as physically abusive unless the life of the child is in jeopardy.

The definition of sexual abuse differs substantively from that of physical abuse. The dynamics of the situation are different, a different type of treatment modality is called for, and the abuses pose quite different problems for the children.

Sexual abuse of a child is the utilization of the child for sexual gratification or an adult's permitting another person to so use the child.

Determining sexual abuse requires much more in the way of judgment, and great latitude in behavior and events are noted. It is clearly sexual abuse when a father has sexual relations with his daughter. But is it abuse if a father does not respect his daughter's desire for privacy while dressing, or if he honestly complains because his daughter, who is entering puberty, no longer wishes to bathe with him? Most people would agree that the second father is an unwise parent, but charging abuse is quite a different matter.

The definition has many limitations: "sexual gratification" as a criterion is usually inferred but cannot be proved. It includes permitting practices that can be criticized on the grounds of contributing to the delinquency of a child, and one adult may be charged in effect with the behavior of another.

Scientific Research

With a few very notable exceptions, sophisticated social scientific research in the field of child abuse is lacking. The most fundamental research guidelines are frequently ignored or overlooked: In much of the research, samples are highly stratified, and through ignorance, the authors label them as random. Some research has not only been based on inadequate samples but also has lacked control groups, which were indicated by the research design.

Also, researchers in the area of child abuse often fall into the sophomoric mistake of believing that correlation implies causation. In everyday terms, we know that it cannot rain without clouds. On the other hand, the presence of clouds does not mean that it will rain. In child abuse, researchers often take the position that because alcohol (an evil) is present, child abuse (another evil) must result. The same can be applied to "hostile feelings" or many other so-called causes of child abuse. Many people use alcohol, and many use it excessively, but that does not mean that they will all abuse their children. Similarly, all of us have "hostile feelings," but that does not mean we are all abusive.

Unfortunately, inadequately designed research projects and data collection can lead to misleading if not false conclusions. One illustration of a data source that may well mislead researchers is the National Standard Form of the National Clearinghouse on Child Neglect and Abuse (see Appendix). This form, distributed to the states in 1974, is the result of a joint effort by the Children's Division of the American Humane Association and the Office of Child Development of the Department of Health, Education, and Welfare.

The form is clearly deficient in seeking needed statistics on child abuse. It does not address itself to the entire population of abusers but only to that segment reported to agencies charged with investigating abuse. It is highly unlikely that the thousands of non-medical personnel in private practice who encounter abusers will report any data and none have been sought from them. This means that the figures do not take into account abusers who can afford private practitioners. The form is specifically biased toward middle-class values. It asks for such information as whether the child was "illegitimate" or the "product of a multiple birth." From a purely research point of view it is a poor tool in that the person filling out the form must make a judgment that is basic to the whole research effort: whether the abuse or neglect is "established," strongly indicated, weakly indicated, or "not substantiated." The form is to be completed if any category other than the last is checked!

The stress on neglect is obvious, and it probably reflects social workers' longtime concerns, although neglect and abuse are quite separate research and treatment problems. Every researcher has an ethical obligation to anticipate how a data collection form will be used and what the consequences may be. It is easy to see how this form could become another means by which public agency workers threaten neglectful parents. If clients do not appear for interviews or change their behavior so that the worker is satisfied, they may well be defined as abusive and reported to a national agency and clearinghouse. In view of the amount of money spent in creating this form and the thousands of hours that will go into completing it in every city and hamlet of this country, it is tragic that skilled, trained social science researchers were not employed to "translate" experiences of practicing social workers into a viable research design.

As in the National Standard Form, many research reports do not define terms and use inadequate and sometimes highly inappropriate statistics, and, in a few instances, researchers have extrapolated from an N of 1 to the entire population. Research is a serious business and a technical one, and it may well be the key to unraveling most of the problems in the field. Yet few people in public and private agencies are qualified to do research, and many programs are funded on hope, with no research or evaluative design as part of the program. We tend to perpetuate the pattern of doing research to "prove" that our program is working, thus we need more money to accomplish our ends. Without sophisticated, sound, basic research, we will not achieve an understanding of child abuse.

We lack theory in the area of child abuse. Our current position is one of multiple causation, which is not a theory. We frequently cite the analytical and pathological models, but they cannot explain the phenomenon. If we are tied to a position that dictates a certain cause, we will assuredly find the theoretical effect. This in turn mandates the use of the ameliorative or treatment strategy of that particular orientation. But most abusive parents are not pathological, and the "social deficiency" school of thought (poverty, discrimination, socioeconomic class) is also inadequate. Most poor people do not abuse their children; most people in the "lower class," whatever that may mean to the researcher, do not abuse their children; and most people who are discriminated against do not abuse their children unless one considers the use of physical force in and of itself as abusive. In that event, we must conclude that most American parents are abusive.

Theory construction is a difficult, tedious, and time-consuming process. It requires definition, delineation, original research that can be replicated by others, testing, modification, and many other things. "Armchair philosophers" have occasionally developed sound theory, but they are few and far between. We will not develop a separate, distinct theoretical base without basic research, and it will require time. Finally, it must be stated that there is a vast difference between data collection and sophisticated research.

One basic theoretical issue that must be resolved is the lack of discrimination among abusers. Many include all abusers under a global definition (and an unclear one at that) and view them as being the same. They are not. There are different types of physical abusers, and sexual abusers of children are quite different from physical abusers. This point is sometimes difficult to understand but it is fairly simple, if a medical analogy is used. The word *cancer* is a general term used to explain an organic process. But there are different types of cancer, just as there are different types of heart problems. The treatment for cancer varies, depending upon the type and location of the diseased or runaway cells. We might also look at the term *transportation,* which includes air, ground, and sea transportation, each using a variety of fuels. At the next level we have the concept of *automobile,* which includes vehicles of different sizes, colors, and models. The point of these analogies is that we are at a rather primitive stage when we speak of "child abuse." There are different types of physical abusers, and with additional information, we will probably find that different types of sexual abusers exist.

CHAPTER FOUR

A Typology of Physical Abusers

As we have seen, the term *child abuse* covers a pattern of behavior by parents that leads to a negative judgment of their child-rearing capabilities or practices. It is generally considered a punitive parental or adult caretaker response, although in accidental abuse or neglect leading to abuse the punishment aspect is not present. In our society, the term *discipline,* which has a more positive connotation, is preferable to *punishment.*

In the layperson's view abuse can be defined by an act or the visible results of an act by an adult against a child. In addition, most laypersons and many professionals tend to judge abuse according to their own individual biases and preferences. In other words, if the perceived severity of parental actions exceeds that degree of force employed by the observer, it is defined as abusive behavior. As one abuser rather cynically stated, "The Judge [who admitted employing a razor strop on his own child] told me he disciplined his child but I punished and abused mine!"

Evaluating other parents on the basis of one's own childhood or parental experiences seems universal. Parents who never use physical force feel that parents who employ an object, such as a hairbrush, belt, or strap, are abusive. Those parents in turn feel that they only "discipline" their children, while the parents who employ heat, fan belts, or cigarette butts are abusive. And so the story goes.

The legalistic view of child abuse concerns itself with matters of proof, *mens rea* (or intent), and issues that favor the parent rather than the child. The law does not clearly define child abuse.

In other types of assault it has been able to define various conducts and degrees of culpability—such as 1st, 2nd, and 3rd degree murder, and assault with or without intent to maim or kill. Beeause child abuse covers many types of behavior, lawyers as well as persons in other disciplines concerned with this national problem are struggling with definitions.

Much of the difficulty stems from the fact that all abusers are lumped into one category, although an examination of parents labeled "abusers" will reveal great differences in motivation, abusive practices, and results. Yet certain commonalities are seen in certain groups of abusers, and these have implications for legislation, treatment, and recovery.

At the moment there is no ongoing systematic, sophisticated research in the field of child abuse. Child abuse has been viewed as symptomatic of other conditions, and its treatment has been based on analytic or other models borrowed from a host of disciplines and "fitted" to child abuse. Data about abusers now being gathered on a nationwide basis will probably be more harmful than beneficial and will mislead the public and the professional community. As Clinard and Quinney (1967) so aptly stated the problem, "It is unlikely that an adequate comprehensive theory of behavior can be readily formulated and identified directly from a heterogeneous mass of phenomena."

McKinney (1966) states that a typology is a "purposive, planned selection, abstraction, and accentuation of a set of criteria with empirical referents that serves as a basis for comparison of empirical cases." If we are to arrive at any theory or formulation in child abuse, we must separate the raw data into discrete types that can be examined and tested.

Several problems arise in typologies constructed from clinical contact: Unequal weights are given unconsciously; formulations are usually based on microscopic samples; and randomness is not considered; to mention a few. Yet, it can be worthwhile (as has been done by Jean Piaget) to extrapolate from a small sample in order to contribute to the general development of knowledge and understanding.

In the typology presented below, sexual abuse and "crossover" (a combination of physical and sexual abuse) are excluded. Physical abusers appear to share many commonalities and represent the bulk of cases brought to the attention of social agencies. Sexual abuse is largely undiscussed, and, while certain trends appear, insufficient data exist for the construction of a typology. Further, sexual abuse is substantively different than physical abuse. The motivation, family dynamics, and treatment are markedly different, and the two kinds of abuse must be discussed as separate rather than intrinsically related phenomena. "Crossover" cases are not unknown, but we have insufficient data to warrant including this phenomenon in the typology.

The following typology is offered for the physical abuser:

1. Socially and parentally incompetent abuser
2. Frustrated and displaced abuser
3. Situational abuser
4. Neglectful abuser
5. Accidental or unknowing abuser
6. Victim-precipitated abuse
7. Subcultural abuser
8. Mentally ill abuser
9. Institutionally prescribed abuse
10. Self-identified abuser

This typology has obvious limitations; foremost among them is the fact that many abusers do not fall clearly within one category and that categories overlap. Still another is that if there are two adult abusers in the home, such as a mother and a father, one may fall within one category and the other may be classified in another. In instances where this typology has been utilized, two professionals viewing a case have placed the same abuser in different classifications.

Clinicians who have used the typology tend to use the second type (Frustrated and displaced abuser) as a "catchall." They do so because they believe that all humans suffer some degree of frustration and because projection is a fairly common defense mechanism. Further, some people seem predisposed to seek frustration and projection as defense mechanisms to the exclusion of all other possibilities. Similarly, when the designation "Severely emotionally disturbed" was substituted for the eighth type (Mentally ill abuser), this category was selected much more frequently. In-depth interviews revealed that "mentally ill" implies psychosis to many, but that "severely emotionally disturbed" (a) gave greater latitude, i.e., to include those who were not psychotic and (b) was utilized when the evaluator was disturbed by and reacted to the object, act, or method employed by the abusive adult.

Despite its limitations, the typology still offers a viable alternative to the practice of putting all abusers in one classification, treating them all the same, and believing that all abuse stems from the same stimulus. With additional research, this typology may offer a basis for the construction of theory and the development of unique treatment models, which are not borrowed from other fields.

The typology also enables professionals to view a situation involving abuse in a more objective manner than is currently the case, and it avoids obvious pitfalls in making value judgments about environmental factors. Specifically, data currently being collected include family income, in an effort to see if poverty exists. Poverty, insofar as it relates to child abuse, is not a matter of income size but the effect and reaction to a perceived lack of money. The author has treated abusers in the $45,000–$75,000 income bracket who had financial problems. In this sense, we might rightly argue that an income of $100,000 per year would have relieved their financial pressure! Similarly, it must be recognized that most parents in the various federal poverty categories (and they do vary widely) do not abuse their children. It is naive to think that raising the level of income will reduce child abuse.

This typology deals only with physical abuse and for the most part ignores the problem of "emotional abuse." This limitation is deliberate, for the difficulties we have in defining physical abuse are multiplied in attempting to define emotional abuse. Who is to judge? And is emotional abuse a matter to which the courts should address themselves?

Probably the greatest emotionally abusive parents are middle-class Americans who withhold love or use the contingency of love to manage their children. If John brings home a report card with five *A*s and one *C* the typical response of middle-class parents is not, "How well you have done!" but, "Why did you get the *C*?" This constitutes emotional abuse. Low grades frequently prompt middle-class parents to set curfew hours and enforced study time and to limit dating; and their children experience feelings of guilt and worthlessness. This, also, is emotional abuse.

Emotional abuse is pandemic in middle-class America, and it often affects children longer and more deeply than physical abuse. Yet, physical abuse can result in the death of a child, and, at this point, a value judgment is made that the preservation of life is more important than attempting to deal with emotional abuse.

Let us now examine each type of physical abuser in the typology.

The Socially and Parentally Incompetent Abuser

The majority of abusers fall into this classification. Being a parent is a learned, rather than inherited, behavior. These abusers are judged socially and parentally incompetent on the basis of a disciplinary practice or series of practices that have been defined as "abusive" in modern society. Most of them are simply utilizing the very same techniques to control children that were used with them by their parents. In this sense, we see an intergenerational pattern, as the following cases will illustrate:

A father hit his 7-year-old son with a 2x4 and fractured the boy's clavicle. The father was reported as an abuser. The victim's grandfather said he literally used to take his son "to the woodshed, just as my father did to me." Here, three generations have used wood to discipline children.

A mother known to the author was serving a prison term for the death of one of her children. She had placed her children in a tub of very hot water to discipline them. She was distracted and left them in the hot water for some time, and one died. The mother's hand and arms bore quite noticeable scars. As a child her mother forced her to put her hands on the stove when she misbehaved. The grandmother of the decedent showed me scars on the backs of her legs; her mother had made her stand against an open hot stovepipe. In this family we see the intergenerational persistence of the use of heat as a disciplinary measure.

One mother tied her daughter to a bed for many hours. She had been tied to a bed when she was a child, as had her mother when she was a child.

With increased concern over child abuse in America, practices that were common in former times are no longer deemed permissible. Did child abuse exist years ago? Certainly it did, but the prevailing attitude was that what parents chose to do to their children was their business. In fact, many elderly people can remember a day in their childhood when a child "down the road" simply disappeared or was buried on the family farm, presumably as the result of parental abuse.

Replication of parental practice is exceedingly common. One learns to be a parent from one's interaction with one's own parents, just as one learns to act like a boy or a girl or to be a spouse by observing the interactions in one's home. Ask any fairly large group of people how often, for what reason, and in what manner they were disciplined as children, and then inquire how they disciplined their own children. A surprisingly high degree of replication can be observed in most groups. Significantly, a few will say that they were punished frequently and severely as children and that they will not strike their own children, and a few will say that they employ more in the way of punishment than was used on them. But this does not negate the basic principle. Analogous to these responses are those of people whose parents were alcoholics; many say that under no circumstances will they ever drink or allow alcohol in their homes.

Exposure, identification, and labeling of the socially and behaviorally incompetent adult abuser is probably a result of changing child-care standards and societal expectations, the continuing shift from rural to urban living, and more "eyes and ears" in each community. We live closer together than in the past, and the crying child or abusive adult can now be heard and seen by many people in an apartment complex, whereas before there was no one to hear. Abused children often come to the attention of the community earlier through day care centers, city recreation programs, law enforcement, and preschool activities. Without a doubt, the old assumption that a child is the parent's property is being systematically challenged. All these factors lead to increased discovery and reporting of this type of abuser, and this trend will continue.

Another phenomenon to which agencies should become attuned is the fact that many Americans are increasingly turning away from violence as a means of resolving problems. This is particularly true among younger people, and many young parents seek, desire, and need help in developing parental mechanisms of a nonviolent nature, which are different from those of their own childhood.

Any behavior that is learned can be unlearned and be replaced by new behavior. Such is the case with disciplinary or punitive practices that are considered abusive. Parents in this category have not been exposed to a wide repertoire of coping mechanisms with their children, and they are particularly good to work with in groups. With professional assistance, many of these parents can and frequently do develop nonabusive behavior in a short period of time.

The Frustrated and Displaced Abuser

All of us have heard the story of the father who yells at the wife, who screams at the child, who kicks the dog or cat. Sadly, there is more truth than fiction to that tale, and many children are abused because they become the targets of parental frustration and aggression. Every human being experiences stress and frustration and has aggressive tendencies, but most of us handle those problems in socially acceptable ways. A few do not and become emotionally crippled, alcoholic, or dependent on other drugs. Even fewer abuse their children.

Most families work out some détente, and the children know

they should not approach Mother with a problem until after her second cup of coffee, or Father until he has read the evening paper. Many families do not, though, because the parents have not identified when they are vulnerable, nor have the children. Still others are so extended in holding two jobs or one highly demanding job, that they are physically tired most of the time and prone to be aggressive toward their children.

The key to treatment of this type of abuser is not as difficult as it may appear. Primarily, the professional's goal is to assist the abuser in identifying the sources of frustration, reducing the frustration if feasible, and "teaching" the abuser to employ defense mechanisms other than displacement.

The Situational Abuser

In many instances, an otherwise nonabusive individual becomes an abusive parent because of a particular situation. Truncated homes or those in which a parent is absent for prolonged periods of time and then reappears seem particularly susceptible to abuse. Frequently a home will function fairly well without the presence of the father, and when he reappears and asserts his authority, it is not well received. A stepparent entering a home is frequently challenged by his or her spouse's children from an earlier marriage, and this can lead to difficulty. The following cases are examples of the situational abuser:

Mrs. M. beat her two older children with a belt in the yard in the presence of neighbors. She was referred to a local agency, where it was learned that this 23-year-old mother had three children in diapers (which she washed by hand) and was married to a former Marine sergeant who expected elaborate dinners and well-scrubbed and polished floors. He did not help her, and she had not been out of the house except to go to the hospital and the doctor for nearly three years. She rarely slept more than three or four hours a night because of the demands on her.

Mr. J., an enlisted man in the Navy, was assigned to carrier duty and was frequently at sea for prolonged periods. His return home was greeted less than enthusiastically by his teen-age son and daughter, as he imposed limits on their comings and goings, which their mother did not. He and his 15-year-old son had an argument after the boy had stayed out past midnight without permission on three consecutive nights. The son sustained a fractured jaw, and the father was reported for abuse.

Mr. and Mrs. H. were "professional students." For seven years their son was cared for largely by babysitters and in semi-institutional settings. When faced with the problems of caring for him during vacations, they both became abusive with the child, and the problem became worse when Mr. H. got a job, leaving Mrs. H. to care for the boy. Although she expressed love and concern for the child, she stated that she had had virtually no contact with him for years. She knew she was abusive and sought help. The child was later placed with his maternal grandmother.

In situational abuse, the attack on the child results from a combination of the parent and the situation itself. Usually if whatever is causing the stress can be relieved, the abuse ceases. There is a great overlap between the frustrated and displaced abuser and the situational abuser. The primary distinction is that with the former, projection of feelings on the child (abuse) is the result of a chronic and consistent pattern of expressing frustration, and in the latter, the situation itself is the primary problem that results in aggression toward the child.

The Neglectful Abuser

This designation should be used only if the life of the child is in danger; that is, if a continuation of the neglectful actions will result in death to the child. Rarely is the social worker or psychologist capable of making this judgment; rather, it falls within the domain of the medical profession. When we think of imminent danger to the life of the child, it is a bit farfetched to define a parent as a neglectful abuser if the child is 6 years old. If persistent inadequate diet were to lead to death, the child would not have survived to that age. Public health nurses are probably the best-qualified resource for the professional trying to make such an assessment, for they encounter many neglectful situations during the course of their normal duties.

To be sure, there are parents who neglect their children to the point where they may be considered abusive, but they are few in number when compared with the total in the category of neglect as used by public agencies. These parents share many commonalities: They are usually poor, uneducated, dependent, unemployed or underemployed, and the product of two or more generations of welfare assistance. Without being patronizing or demanding, we may say that many function much like small children, and this behavior has been reinforced by contacts with agency caseworkers over many years. In this sense, the abuse occurs because parents who function like 3-year-olds have the responsibility for other 3-year-olds, who happen to be their children. Many times, the adult mother expects the child to "mother" her.

The abuse label is probably the one most misused by professionals. Caseworkers or teachers will define a parent as a neglectful abuser because the children have dirty or insufficient clothing or lack an adequate diet (i.e., without fruit or meat, which is beyond the financial capability of many families). Or the labeling is the judgment of one person, who neither understands nor accepts life styles and values different from his or her own.

In many instances it is the social agencies not the parents that should be called "abusive." There is no justification for labeling people neglectful or abusive because their plumbing is unsanitary or lacking altogether or because they give their children dog food to eat. (It is estimated that one out of every three cans of dog food sold in the inner city is consumed by humans.) The label of "abuser" should not be placed on the parent but on the society that permits these conditions to exist and on the agencies that fund personnel to complete reports in triplicate but divert no funds to the purchase of needed plumbing, bedding, or food.

The following cases may help to illustrate the category of the neglectful abuser:

Mr. B., age 23, and Mrs. B., age 19, have two infants. Never employed, both were dependent on public assistance and did not manage that money well. They were unresponsive to the efforts of the public assistance worker who was concerned about the children. When the public health nurse accompanied her on a home visit, they found the children in a crib alone and unattended. Both had open sores, and one child was literally being chewed on by a large rat. Both were emaciated and required hospitalization.

Mary was a 2-year-old child who had convulsions, which became increasingly severe and frequent. Both her mother and her mother's boyfriend said that "fits" were "common in the family and no one took anything." The mother stated that Mary would "outgrow the fits." Physicians disagreed and insisted on anticonvulsant medication. The mother "kept forgetting" to give Mary the medication, and for Mary's protection, the authorities sought and received custody of the child.

An 82-year-old blind and senile grandmother, for the most part bedridden, was found with a three-month-old child. She stated that she thought, "I'll just keep her until my granddaughter gets through marketing." A neighbor stayed with the grandmother and cared for the child for three hours before calling the authorities. Social work investigators located the mother of the child, who stated she placed the infant with her grandmother three days prior to discovery. The child had been given only water during that time.

Miss A. lived with her two sons in a shack with no plumbing. She was dependent for her support on a series of "boyfriends" and a small county welfare grant. Chickens, dogs, and cats inhabited the house along with the three members of the family. Defecation and urination in the yard and small garden were commonplace.

Mr. and Mrs. J. are the third generation of a family on welfare. Neither one works, but Mr. J. has hopes of starting a car repair business. At least, that is his explanation for having four junked cars in his yard. He also has three refrigerators in need of repair which he will fix "someday" and sell. His three children have the freedom of the yard. During a home visit by the social worker, one child was missing. The social worker fortunately found the child inside a closed refrigerator.

Clearly each of these children's lives was in jeopardy. The motivation of the parent is really of no consequence. What is important is the expectation that practices that threaten the life of the child will continue. With their concern for the safety of the child, professionals need not burden themselves or the parents with terms such as "dilapidated housing," "disinterested and slovenly parents," and other similar descriptions so often found in the naming of certain parents as neglectful abusers.

This position in no way minimizes the effects of continued or prolonged neglect that does not threaten the life of the child. Neglect is a major problem facing most public welfare and family service agencies, and it occupies a large percentage of staff time and effort. However, there is no reason to handicap these parents further by labeling them abusive.

The Accidental or Unknowing Abuser

Although it is rare, some parents are unaware that they are abusing their children. Extremely poor parental judgment due to limited intelligence can result in the death or injury of a child. Some practitioners feel that mentally or socially retarded parents should be included in this category along with "apathetic parents." When abuse occurs in these situations, the community will frequently "excuse" the parental behavior, particularly if it has been known to the community for some time. The following are some examples of this type of abuser:

Mr. B. was a "quick draw" artist with a pistol and held several trophies to prove it. He encouraged his son to follow his hobby and permitted him to practice with him. The son was 5. During practice, the son shot himself in the leg, and he nearly died from loss of blood.

Mr. and Mrs. T. were professional swimmers and divers. They prided themselves on teaching very young children to swim, and they taught their 3-year-old to dive from great heights. During one practice, the child hit the bottom of the pool and was killed. Mr. T. was imprisoned.

Mrs. R. was a successful, well-respected surgical nurse. She was divorced and had three sons, who were active and outgoing. To discipline them, she would administer enemas to them. She freely admitted this to the pediatrician, seeing nothing wrong with the practice, "as it did not hurt them and it might even help." The pediatrician, noting that the children would sometimes receive enemas daily, referred Mrs. R. to the author as an abuser.

A couple met in an institution for the mentally retarded and later married and had children. Difficulties began while the mother was in the hospital, as she had no idea of child care or much concern with learning. To her, children were quite literally "little dolls." Both parents expressed love for the children but were incapable of providing care. Complaints from neighbors and relatives eventually resulted in permanent placement of the children.

In each instance, damage to the child was the result of action or inaction due to parental inadequacy, poor judgment, or emotional/physical disability. Parents in this category usually do not continue to abuse after professional intervention. Sometimes, one set of circumstances results in praise for the child and parent and another leads to condemnation. After all, if William Tell had been less accurate with his bow and arrow, he would have killed his son!

Victim-Precipitated Abuse

To professionals in the field, it is a well-known fact that some children seem to precipitate abusive and aggressive behaviors in adults. This is difficult for the layperson to accept because of cultural bias and myth that children are "innocent." Indeed, the very concept of protective services has arisen because children cannot fend for themselves and need protection from adults. This emotional set— that children are innocent victims, helpless against adult aggressors— precludes many from examining the dynamics of the child involved.

When one child in a family is targeted, the most frequent explanation given is that of an analytical model. Common explanations are that the child reminds the parent of a former spouse, a hated parent, or of the abuser's own childhood (always unpleasant). Subscribing to such an explanation, many professionals then feel that the abusive parent is "sick," and that the resolution of the abuse will come if the adult will explore those feelings, develop insights, and act upon those insights. The explanation of the targeted child, however, does not rest in the analytic model. Let us first view a few cases:

John, age 5, was the third child in a family of four and was the only child who was abused. The father and mother discussed the situation with a minister, who referred them to a local mental health clinic. The abuse continued, and the parents requested that John be placed in temporary (foster) care. Three weeks after John was admitted to the emergency room after a severe beating by his foster father. The foster father had never harmed a child before, and his home was considered one of the better placements in the county. He was extremely upset over having beaten John and stated, "He is so whiney I just couldn't take it anymore." While in the pediatric ward of the local hospital, John was described by nurses as "demanding and not too lovable."

Annette was one of three children in the family and the only one abused. At age 2 she was described as "cute," at 2½ as "mischievous," and by age 3 was a "troublemaker who will not respond to anything except spankings." She would deliberately antagonize her parents by breaking things, not eating, and engaging in other behavior that was in direct contrast to that of her siblings. A list of her negative behavior would be handed to the father upon his arrival home, and abuse would ensue. In observing family interaction, it was obvious that praise was given to the siblings for their accomplishments and negative rewards were given to Annette. No positive or desired behavior of this child was reinforced.

Edward was 7, introspective, quiet, and read a lot. He did not care for the outdoor life of his two older brothers and his father, who "lives for outdoor activities." Frequently taunted by his brothers and father as a "sissy," Edward began to break fishing rods, lines, and other equipment. When he was caught by his father in the act of cutting a hole in a tent, he was severely beaten and was denied food for three days.

In each of these situations the child was selected for abuse for different reasons. Most common in victim-precipitated abuse is the reinforcement not of desired behavior but of undesired behavior. A common-sense explanation of how the child develops in this manner might be seen in a child tugging at a parent for attention. If the parent is reading a newspaper and does not wish to be disturbed and strikes the child, that behavior of the child is reinforced. The alternative is no parental attention, and in the child's mind, attention for misbehavior is better than no attention at all.

The Subcultural Abuser

Within American society we have many subcultures, some that place an inherent positive value on doing violence to children and some that abuse children in order to accomplish other ends. Subculture does not refer to racial or ethnic groups, but to values and to subgroups in society that include members of every race, income group, and social class.

Perhaps the most common abuse in this category is that perpetrated on religious grounds. Using the Old or the New Testament, one could justify the abuse of children as worthy and desirable in the development of a "good Christian." It should be noted, however, that some people will deduce one course of action from reading a passage, while others will arrive at a quite different conclusion.

Wolfgang and Ferracuti (1967) wrote of a "sub-culture of violence," and pointed out that a violence response to certain stimuli was demanded if one subscribed to the values of that subculture. This type of subculture is found particularly in the southeastern United States among certain groups, but the value is by no means universally accepted in that geographical area. Members of this subculture have migrated to other parts of the country, and we find some people in nearly every large city who subscribe to violence as a means of resolving interpersonal problems. Indeed, one could easily make a case that this particular subculture is only an extension of our country's use of violence to resolve both foreign and domestic problems. We often hear that abused children grow up to be violent, and become criminals and murderers. Children who do probably come from this type of abuse situation. Frequently their forebears and family have been involved in crime partly as a way of life, and they learned violence at an early age through continuous examples.

There also seems to exist a myth in America, based on the "spare the rod and spoil the child" theory, that if we do not physically punish children they will turn out to be criminals. This myth needs exploring. In 1972, while the author was serving as a consultant to a state department of corrections, one of his responsibilities was to work with some twenty men sentenced to be executed. Most of them had been severely punished and beaten in childhood. Not one related that "the rod was spared." To anyone working in corrections it is abundantly clear that violence does indeed beget violence.

In one state, authorities were asked to investigate a child-caring institution that had the responsibility for over 150 children. It was operated by a minister of a fundamentalist sect but was not recognized by the sect. The authorities found the children well fed, well dressed, and well housed, but beatings with fan belts and other instances of abuse were quite common. When asked why these practices were permitted, the superintendent responded, "It says in the Bible, 'suffer unto me little children.' "

In another state, a father accused by school officials of abusing his three sons appeared in the local family services office with a large whip wrapped around his waist to contest the complaint. He admitted severely punishing his sons to "make them good Christians" and wanted precise and specific information from the protective services worker on exactly what the law permitted in the way of objects that could be used against his sons.

Mr. P., who was described to the author by a social worker as "white trash," was reported for physically abusing his 5-year-old son and 3-year-old stepson. Mr. P. volunteered that he had served a term in prison for attempted murder, carried a knife, and was unemployed more often than not. His rationale in abusing his sons was "to toughen them up and make them men."

The Mentally Ill Abuser

It is not uncommon for the layperson to feel that all adults who abuse children are mentally ill. News reports about obviously pathological persons who abuse their children reinforce this myth, but these adults are newsworthy simply because of their behavior. Most professionals working with abusers agree that the mentally ill abuser is statistically in the minority.

Abuse by the mentally ill should be considered a symptom of the illness rather than an end in itself. The prognosis for these abusers varies, but they often abuse children again even after hospitalization. In part, this is because of the manner in which most hospitals treat mental illness, which is by pharmacological symptom control. Patients are hospitalized, medicated, and released in relatively short order. When they do not continue taking their medication they again become ill and abuse their children, and sometimes they abuse even while taking medication.

The poor prognosis of some mentally ill abusers is recognized, and at most seminars dealing with child abuse one or more case histories are cited that indicate (a) long-standing mental illness in the adult, (b) continued abuse of children, and (c) the need for termination of parental rights and adoptive placement of the children. This reasoning, however, overlooks the fact that the symptoms rather than the illness are being pharmacologically managed and that most mentally ill abusers come to society's attention in their early twenties and have nearly twenty years of possible child bearing before them. Termination and placement of one or two children does not solve the problem. In fact, in some cases mentally ill mothers have rather defiantly stated they would have more children as soon as possible after termination. Children bolster a parent's self-concept and are an extension of the adult.

Mrs. L., a 23-year-old mother, forced her daughter, age 1½, to eat feces, which she called "God's food." Her husband, 25, was in the hospital for mental illness, and Mrs. L. had been in and out of mental institutions since she was 16. The abuse of the child was referred to the local mental health clinic, where Mrs. L. was being seen. Three months later the child was killed because, in Mrs. L.'s words, her daughter was "the Devil."

Mr. B. had been committed to the hospital three times. Each commitment had been preceded by bizarre, destructive behavior. A neighbor who heard screams, found Mr. B. burning his son with a blowtorch. When the police were called, he threatened to kill the child and himself if they tried to return him to the hospital. When the police arrived he committed suicide with a shotgun.

Mrs. F. and her six-month-old daughter were found by a relative who had not seen them for several days. Mrs. F. was completely withdrawn and "in a catatonic stupor." The child obviously had not been fed for more than twenty-four hours and required hospitalization.

Although the prognosis is poor for a number of mentally ill

abusers, for others it is very good. Many can and have been helped. Successful treatment of the mentally ill abuser is usually a fairly long process, requiring a large investment of time on the part of a team of professionals drawn from many disciplines and agencies.

Institutionally Prescribed Abuse

The striking, spanking, humiliation, and harming of children in public and private schools, day care centers, detention homes, orphanages, and correctional facilities probably represents a greater part of the problem of child abuse than is admitted, discussed, or reported. Abuse is tolerated in many instances by state welfare departments because they license these facilities and are emotionally committed to working with the personnel, primarily administrators, in hopes of effecting some change. Succinctly, one worker in the licensing division of a state department said to the author, "We know full well that she [the proprietor of a day care facility] is hurting the children, but we really need day care centers!"

The following are examples of institutionally prescribed abuse:

In a center for the mentally retarded, children were frequently beaten by attendants for infractions of rules that most of them could not comprehend. Many were forced into painful positions that could be injurious to their health. The administrator's explanation was, "At the salaries we pay, we just can't recruit good attendants."

In a day care center, children who misbehaved were locked in a closet and denied food. If they defecated while in the closet, additional punishment was inflicted. Children as young as a year and a half were beaten for urinating in their diapers.

Literally hundreds of examples, most far worse than the ones cited, can be found in the United States. The unfortunate fact is that when these practices are exposed, the general public feels that they represent a minuscule minority and are the result of the children's "bringing it on themselves." Only through education will this attitude change, and the public will learn that it is not just a "few bad apples in a barrel" but that many of the barrels are rotten.

In one sense, institutionally prescribed abuse is the most insidious and horrible of all. It is administered without feeling, for the violation of a rule, and does not occur until long after the rule has been violated. Many school boards even have regulations that insure that the punishment is not administered with any emotion or feeling. The evils of these practices are many, and from a human standpoint it becomes easier to understand the parent or adult who lashes out at a child in anger than the adult principal who assaults a child in a cold, dispassionate, and premeditated manner.

In state prisons, if an officer assaults an adult felon, in all probability his or her employment will be terminated, and criminal charges may be brought. But in local elementary schools, teachers can and do employ physical violence against children. It seems rather odd that we can manage prisons housing more than a thousand murderers, rapists, and thieves but cannot manage a kindergarten of twenty-five children without hitting them. If we employ violence as a means of solving problems in schools, it would only seem consistent for principals to strike teachers for infractions of the rules!

In fairness to the schools, however, we must recognize that many children resent school and that the schools are being called upon to manage more and more children with less and less staff. Most teachers know that physical punishment is the least effective means of controlling children. Many would prefer to develop meaningful, consistent reinforcement schedules as a positive means of handling children, but they lack the expertise to do so. In the not too distant future, courses in the area of reinforcement scheduling for children will become a necessity in teacher training colleges and universities.

Institutionally prescribed abuse in settings other than schools will be more difficult to eliminate because of the lack of public scrutiny, the feeling (fostered by administrators and fund raisers) that these institutions are in effect the parents of the children in residence and therefore have the parental prerogative of doing violence to them, and the relationship between the social workers who issue state licenses and the institutional social workers and administrators. In fact, some young, aggressive social workers charged with licensing functions have found a real timidity, bordering on misfeasance, among administrators whose responsibility it is to approve the withholding of a license. At this point, the prevailing attitude in many state agencies is that an institution is entitled to a license unless it can be proved it is not. The burden of proof then is on the state agency rather than the applicant.

Other factors bearing upon the continuation of abuse in child caring institutions are politics and the very licensing laws themselves. In some states a licensee may insure the continuance of the license in the next gubernatorial administration by judicious political donations or services, nor is it unknown for institutional administrators to be appointed to welfare boards that oversee the licensing function! Licensing laws are usually vague and weak. Few carry penalties other than nonrenewal, and, in this instance, an institution can close for a few days, reopen under a new name, and continue business as usual—of which abuse of children is a part.

A drastic solution to the problem of continual relicensing of institutions that abuse children would be to remove the licensing function from state departments of public welfare. That will be unnecessary, however, if strong laws are enacted and public employees are given support in enforcing these laws. Appeal procedures can and should be an integral part of the licensing process to protect the applicant, but the situation must change.

The Self-Identified Abuser

The parents who by their own admission abuse their children are never discussed. The first nine categories consist of adult caretakers who are identified and labeled as abusive by others. The author first came in contact with self-identified abusers as the result of a newspaper story on child abuse. The article listed various community resources concerned with child abuse and ended by stating that if no other resource were available, the reader should feel free to call the author at his university office. As a result of this article, in a community of 60,000, twenty-two persons called. Eighteen ended up in two treatment groups of nine each.

Self-identified abusers are aware that if their child-rearing practices were known to the community, they would be censured. Because of their self-perception of their social and occupational status or because of fear of reprisals, many will not seek help. This population of abusers is not known in the community: They are usually well educated, of high social status, and aware of their difficulties in child rearing. To illustrate this category, let us view a few cases known to the author.

Mrs. K. is the wife of a physician. She contacted the author and stated that she had broken her 3-year-old son's arm four months earlier by twisting it in a "fit of anger." Medical records verified that the child had in fact been treated for a broken arm in the emergency room of the local hospital. Mrs. K. "hinted" at abuse and was given three plausible and acceptable "explanations" as to how the fracture could have occurred by an emergency room physician with whom she and her husband socialized. After contacting the author, her husband refused to seek help and stated, "If it were ever known, my practice would suffer."

Mr. J., dean of a college in a large midwestern university, is bright and articulate. He contacted the author because he placed high expectations on his son, and when the son would not or could not achieve to that level, Mr. J. would, in his own words, "beat him unmercifully and sometimes burn him with a cigarette." His wife also "gets carried away."

Mr. L. is a successful real estate broker who works sixteen to eighteen hours a day. Over the past six months he noticed an increasing frequency of bruises and cuts on his daughter, age 4. Initially feeling that his daughter was "accident prone," he returned home unexpectedly at 10 A.M. and "caught" his wife beating the child with a hairbrush. He denied any awareness that this was occurring prior to discovery.

Mr. U. is a 28-year-old foreign graduate student working on an advanced degree. He states, "Things are different in America, and we punish our children as we wish back home." He feared reporting of his practice of tying his children to a chair for hours as punishment.

Self-identified abusers seem to share certain characteristics: They are considered socially and professionally "successful," they are acutely aware of the possible consequences that may arise from a continuation of the abuse, and they are highly motivated to solve the problem. They also seem to have an aversion to going to traditional or established agencies such as welfare departments, mental health centers, or family service agencies. This resistance stems in part from the agency images and their fear of a violation of confidentiality. They are afraid that going for treatment for abuse may become known to the community, particularly the professional sector.

The self-identified abuser also poses problems for the professional. With compulsory reporting laws, professionals receiving a plea for help by these troubled parents either violate the law, draw the mantle of professional privilege around themselves, or report the case, in effect, betraying the patient.

From a research point of view, we need more information about this group of people, who thus far have remained hidden.

CHAPTER FIVE

Some Alternatives to Current Treatment Practices

It is an open secret among professionals that we are doing little, if anything, to treat abusers within our current structure. Treatment programs are outmoded, inefficient, extremely expensive, and unworkable. In part that is because they are based on a philosophy developed in a cumbersome bureaucracy originating in the 1930s. Most agencies view the "client," "patient," or "deviant" as "hopeless," or nearly so, and as inferior to the person working on the "case." They feel that only through authoritarian and punitive threats, coupled with a reward here and there, will people change. They do not work "with" a person, although their rhetoric says they do. Working "with" someone implies mutual acceptance, give-and-take, and that one person (the professional) will have impact on the other (the client or patient). It also implies that the client or patient will in turn have impact on and in some way change the professional. Current agency efforts in child abuse involve working "at" or "to" someone, with the rather naive belief that the client will change or will abide by predetermined socially desirable goals or behavior while the professional will not change at all. In candor, some agencies attempt, under the guise of working with someone, to "work around" the individual through coercion and manipulation.

From the 1930s to the 1960s the people receiving the ministrations of professionals employed in agencies were prepared and thoroughly conditioned to be compliant on the surface, though passively resistant to the whole process. In the late 1960s, at a time of change in many other movements, the "inferior" client/patients rebelled against the "superior" professionals and demanded to be treated as human beings. Some even had the temerity to start welfare rights organizations. The very inclusion of the term *rights* implied that they had none in their dealings with agencies. Subtle changes in outward appearances occurred and are occurring in agencies in dealing with certain groups. A usual response, if they become too demanding or articulate, is to employ the dissidents as paraprofessionals, thus incorporating them into the structure, again in an inferior position, albeit a paid one.

Parents and adults who abuse their children are not organized, nor do they represent a significant portion of the caseload of most agencies charged with the investigation and treatment of abuse. Some pressure has been exerted by self-identified abusers through Parents Anonymous, but this group is not within the existing agency power structure. As a consequence, those designated as "abusive" are largely impotent in determining their own destiny and in demanding that they not be treated as inferiors. Further, in many abuse situations, legal penalties are held in abeyance, thus compounding the problem. We see then a replication of the structure and feelings of the 1930–1960 model, which believes that the abuser is in some way deficient or inferior and that the agency will "correct" that inferiority, thus making the adult nonabusive. In turn, the person designated as "abusive" is reacting in a manner similar to that of many welfare clients of the 1930–1960 era. They passively but effectively resist participation in this demeaning and degrading process, in which they must genuflect to the authority and wisdom of superior human beings who may well control their fate and destiny. Typically, the control is not subtle.

The current practice of "plugging in" child abuse to existing bureaucratic programs, philosophies, and treatment strategies is understandable. It is much more convenient to establish another bureau or department, which addresses itself to child abuse, than to question whether it belongs in an agency at all. Human nature being what it is, vested interests will attempt to convince legislators and the public of the merit of existing practices, personnel, and programs in order to continue the program and increase the funding. This benefits only the agency and the personnel. It does virtually nothing for the abusers.

Throughout the United States the usual steps in handling abuse complaints are: (1) referral to an agency designated by law to receive complaints, (2) home visit by a publicly employed social worker, (3) investigation of the complaint, (4) taking the social history, (5) monthly reports of any changes in the family situation (income, people entering or leaving the home, increase or decrease of monies, etc.), (6) possible and probable placement of the child in foster care, (7) possible referral to another agency, (8) recording of "process," (9) occasional court appearances, and (10) returning the child to the home or closing the case if the family moves over the county line or out of the state.

This procedure is not treatment of abuse. It is a recording of changes in family situations. Let us now look at current common policies, practices, and attitudes and some alternatives based on a new approach and philosophy.

The Determination of Abuse

The finding that child abuse does or does not exist is now determined largely by the investigator's biases, views, prejudices, and philosophy of appropriate child-rearing practices. But professional, rather than personal, judgment as to the existence or nonexistence of abuse can and should be made on the basis of five factors:

1. *Laws Governing Abuse.* Every state has one or more laws which legally define abusive acts. While many of these laws are vague, they do provide the professional with a general idea of what sort of behavior is prohibited.

2. *Prevailing Community Norms.* Regional differences exist regarding permissible and nonpermissible child-rearing practices. Differences also exist among ethnic and nationality groups, among re-

ligious groups, and between rural and urban areas. What may be acceptable in one area may not be tolerated in another. This is true not only of disciplinary practices but of children's behavior as well. What may be considered insolence in a child by one group may be considered normal healthy development in another.

3. *Agency Definition.* Most public and private agencies that receive abuse referrals or work with abuse cases formulate official and unofficial guidelines as to what constitutes "abuse" for their agency. These guidelines frequently evolve over years as the result of policy determination, workloads, and agency focus.

4. *The Abuser.* While it is true that most parents who are labeled "abusers" feel that they are not, it is not uncommon to hear parents in therapy or treatment express concern about their own behavior. Denial, shock, and anger in adults accused of abusing a child are normal and expected, for they are aware that a representative of society is judging them less than adequate as parents. More important is the fact that although they employ brutal practices with their children, the vast majority know that society disapproves of the abuse, even though their motivation (concern for the child) may be acceptable.

5. *The Abusee.* Frequently overlooked or dismissed, is the child's perception of abuse or the act that occurred. A professional working with abuse quickly learns that most abused children do not feel they have been mistreated. Conversely, there are children who feel abused but in the judgment of the worker are not. They and their parents need assistance.

To make the determination that child abuse does or does not exist on the basis of known and observable trauma to the child to the exclusion of all other factors is ludicrous. And for one person to decide whether or not abuse has occurred according to his or her own beliefs about what is "proper" child rearing is even more absurd, for that decision will be based on one or two selective factors. This is not to say a child whose arm or leg has been broken intentionally has not been abused, nor does it imply that certain punitive practices are not universally condemned by American parents. But it remains a gross and highly subjective way of defining the problem, and a way that should be abandoned.

The Pathological Model

Current theory maintains that the physical and sexual abuse of children is due to individual pathology, that the pathological condition must be diagnosed, and that following diagnosis, if there is (a) the development of insight and (b) the alleviation of contributory factors, then (c) the abuse will cease. Coupled with this is the belief that (d) the professional knows why the abuse occurred and (e) the abuser does not. However, the thesis that most abusers are "pathological" in a clinical sense must be challenged. So must points (a) through (e), which depend on that basic premise. The very term *pathology,* borrowed from the field of medicine, implies a disease, a sickness, or a malady. It also implies that the professional is capable of discovering and distinguishing the pathological condition, is capable of treating it, and does not suffer from the same affliction.

A diagnosis of "child abuse" is a negative label. Rather than diagnose "what is wrong" we might investigate the affirmative alternative of "what is right" or "healthy." The most skilled therapists, regardless of their discipline or training, work with the strengths the patient brings to the treatment process. Rather than state that we are faced with a socially cancerous (pathological) child abuser, it seems far better to address ourselves to the relative health of the patient and his or her readiness and capability for the needed therapy.

In many settings, the goal is "insight" into the problem of why the adult abuses the child. With newly achieved insights, the patient then becomes more comfortable with himself, realizes why he abused in the past, and no longer has the need to abuse in the future. This process is time-consuming and expensive. Unfortunately, one can achieve insight on the whys and wherefores of one's behavior and still kill a child, as the author has seen, or one can still maim the child even though one's lot in life has improved. Agencies should subscribe to a very basic goal, which might be stated as, "No more abuse to the child." While the goal is clear, direct, and simple, most agencies have this as a long-range goal rather than an immediate one; the priorities should be reversed.

Superiority of the Therapist

The superior position of the therapist in relation to that of the abuser must be challenged. This attitude is related to the pathological model and is also borrowed from the field of medicine, in which the physician is assumed to be superior to the patient. (In physical pathology the surgeon may remove an arm, a leg, a tumor, or some other afflicted part of the body, but in human behavior the basic conditions and symptoms are usually masked through pharmacological agents.) The medical model does not hold true in the treatment of child abuse, and should be abandoned. The alternative—involvement with and commitment to the abuser—demands more of the therapist, but in the long run, it will prove to be the most effective treatment model.

A number of sensitive administrators of social agencies are aware of the problem of the long-standing treatment attitudes of their staff and of the behavior of some toward abusers. But change is not easy and cannot be accomplished by a written statement from an administrator recommending that new means and methods of treatment be explored. The resistance to change stems from the personal values and backgrounds of the professionals, the training of professionals to see pathology in any human problem situation, the comfort of tradition, and the very nature of the bureaucracy itself.

Many professionals involved in the treatment of physically and sexually abusive adults are aware of the failure of existing programs and treatment strategies. Yet in developing and experimenting with new treatment strategies, they are often faced with disapproval, if not outright disaffection, by older, more experienced professionals. More often than not, it is the recent graduate who is eager to try new ideas and experiments with new techniques. The inevitable failures that some workers experience with abusive adults, coupled with the existing values within their agencies, cause many to adopt the old values and become new additions to an old, outworn philosophy. It need not be so, if we reevaluate our methods.

Distinguishing between Types of Abusers

According to traditional attitudes, child abusers are a distinct entity, they share the same aetiological factors, can be treated similarly, have the same symptoms, and respond best to long-term casework and psychotherapy. But in actual fact, all abusers are *not* the same. They differ substantially from each other, have differing causative factors, and respond to different treatment strategies. Sexual abuse is quite different from physical abuse and more difficult to treat, and the traditional agency model of long-term casework is the method of habit and convenience, not effectiveness.

The alternative to existing, inefficient programs involves discriminating among types of abusers, differentiating among causative factors, and employing an ameliorative strategy based on the adults and children involved. We must begin looking at the human element involved in abuse, and stress treatment models that meet human, rather than organizational, needs. A viable alternative is to retain the skills associated with casework and psychotherapy and eliminate much of their meaningless superstructure. This implies a working with, rather than a working to or at, the abuser and the abused child.

The Cost Element

Since the abuse of children may result in death, it has long been felt that the cost of treatment and cost accountability should not be determinants in treatment. But timeworn, inefficient, and ineffective techniques must now be abandoned. Research does not support the notion that advanced degrees result in more effective treatment, nor is there any real evidence that one-to-one therapy or treatment is consistently more effective or even as effective as other treatment approaches.

In therapy as well as in administration, we must move toward both cost analysis and management by objectives. The objective in working with abusers should be basic and fundamental: a cessation of the physical or sexual abuse. Any other factor is extraneous to the legal, social, and ethical obligation of the agency charged with treatment of the problem.

In the matter of cost analysis, we must recognize the relationship between tax dollars and the effectiveness of the treatment. We must begin to "cost out" professional time and services. It is very expensive for the taxpayers when social workers make home visits. The hourly rates paid to professionals should not be wasted on time spent driving a car. Social welfare administrators currently reward "driving behavior" by giving their staff mileage allowances of 10, 12, even 15 cents per mile. Instead of a flat rate, the rate should decrease with increased mileage to encourage more office interviews.

We must consider working with groups as an economical and efficient alternative to individual services. Group treatment methods can serve more people at a lower per-person cost. If we consider an agency's overhead—rent or building acquisition cost; utilities; janitorial services; administrative, supervisory, secretarial, and professionals' salaries and fringe benefits; office supplies and equipment; service contracts; ad infinitum—the cost of seeing a client is probably a minimum of $50 per hour. Several agency administrators have suggested in private that the cost is more likely $100–$200 per hour or more.

Home Interviews

The whole matter of home visitation needs to be challenged. Contact in the home when an initial complaint is received is sometimes (but not always) necessary. But except for that instance, abusers should be seen in the offices of the professionals working with them. Many abusers can and have been treated without professionals' ever entering their homes, just as the vast majority of other social afflictions can be treated without home visits. Further, most home visits are motivated by the authoritarian needs of agencies or personnel, rather than with any treatment aspect in mind. Abusers usually interpret home visits as "spying" and interference, and, if anything, they only exacerbate their distrust of the "helping professionals." Those who believe that abusers are unmotivated and must have services taken to their homes might well ponder whether unmotivated, unreceptive persons would accept ministrations anywhere. The perhaps startling alternative of office visits can succeed when a healthy relationship is established between the abuser and the professional. With abusers who are unable or unwilling to develop such relationships, authority and other factors within the criminal justice system can be used constructively—when absolutely necessary—to prod them into keeping their office appointments.

The practice of keeping in touch by telephone should be more fully investigated. In many respects it is better to call daily and talk for five minutes about the pressures and the children's behavior during the last twenty-four hours than to see a person weekly or monthly. When there is no telephone in the home, an agency that is serious about providing service should install one. The monthly rental would be far less than the cost of one home visit, and the abuser (and the children) could be contacted on a daily basis.

A final, compelling reason for abandoning home visits is that they have no relationship to treatment. There is no connection between cleanliness (as perceived by the visitor) or planting a garden or removing the 1965 auto on cinder blocks from the front yard and alterations in child-rearing practices.

Group Treatment

Although group methods are rarely used in public agencies, they offer not only a more economical but also a more effective means of treating adult physical abusers. In common-sense terms, one person meeting with a group of eight to ten persons for ninety minutes once a week will actually see as many patients in that hour and a half as another professional who sees individual patients for 50-minute interviews throughout an eight-hour work day. The individual interview was pioneered by mental health professionals and was adopted by public service agencies. It is interesting to note that mental health centers are deeply involved in the use of group techniques, while public agencies cling tenaciously to a less effective technique.

In many state and county public agencies "casework" consists only of reporting changes in a bulky file, and caseloads of 50 to 150 or 200 are not uncommon. Abusers are rarely seen more than once a month. This is not a treatment relationship; agencies can and should inform their constituency that treatment of abusers under these circumstances is impossible.

In one-to-one treatment relationships, the maximum number of abusive patients that any professional can work with effectively is 25. In group treatment, 40 abusers (five groups of 8 or four groups of 10) are probably the outside limit.

In the beginning phase of therapy, in many cases the members of the triad need to be seen or at least contacted by phone daily. In the second phase they should be seen weekly, and in the final phase monthly interviews or contacts are indicated.

Resistance to Help

Popular belief has it that abusive adults are unmotivated and resistive, and therefore must be told forcefully and directly what they must do and how. Initially, real and suspected abusers are in fact resistive, and rather than being unmotivated, their motivation consists of avoiding the agency and the professionals within it.

We must recognize that a stigma is attached to the term "child abuse," which is usually interpreted by the abuser as saying, at best, that he or she is a terrible parent and, at worst, that he or she does not love the child and may cause further harm. If we can accept the fact that resistance and defensiveness are normal reactions, we can then move to the matter of relationships and patient movement.

We must abandon the notion that we can forcefully and directly order clients to do (or not do) certain things. To order an abusive adult to stop abusing is much less effective than a physician's ordering a patient to stop smoking. Physicians have had some success with this means, but no instance has come to the author's attention where it has been effective in getting abusers to cease striking children.

We must instead stress the formation of relationships that will be the basis for change. We must involve ourselves with the abusers if they are to trust us with their feelings. This implies respect for the persons we are working with and a caring and sharing relationship. This does not imply acceptance of the abusive act, but of the person.

We must convey that feeling and mean it. For example, while we do not always accept the behavior our children display, we do love them.

To implement this alternative in spirit and fact will change many practices. Professionals should not turn up unannounced for a "home visit," and they should cease the odious practice of calling their clients by their first names while expecting the abusers to address them formally.

Confidential Areas

Many professionals believe that sexual attitudes and behaviors, along with child-rearing practices, are very private matters, and, accordingly, they should not be discussed and if discussed, should be approached obliquely. The truth is that sexual abuse cannot be treated without discussing sex, and in some depth; and physical abuse of children is usually directly related to child-rearing practices, which must also be discussed.

We must recognize that we are attempting to help, not harm people, and that our relationship is both professional and confidential. A practical alternative is to train personnel to deal with sexual problems, or if such training is not available, to refer cases of sexual abuse to private practitioners under purchase-of-service agreements or to local mental health agencies. In the matter of physical abuse, contrary to the views of many professionals, parents whose difficulties in child rearing are labeled "abuse" want to discuss the topic, provided they have a meaningful relationship with the therapist.

Payment for Services

Until recently it has been felt that abusive adults could not and should not pay for services such as foster care or medical treatment for injuries inflicted by the abuser and that payment for such services was inimical to treatment. But the time has come to subscribe to the notion that "sometimes good medicine tastes bad"; specifically, we must begin to charge parents for professional services.

If parents physically abuse their children and medical care is required, the parents should pay all or at least some of the bill. Even if the family is on public assistance, some financial payment, even if it is only a nickel a week, is necessary, indicated, and of therapeutic value. In one instance a public assistance client caused brain damage to his child. The hospital bill was $13,000. The client paid 25 cents per week, which would not begin to cover the interest, but he was tied directly to his act and the consequences of that act.

Parents should also pay part or all of the cost of foster care for their children. Whenever possible, it is preferable to remove the abusers from the home instead of the children. It is remarkable how many parents who "cannot afford to live anywhere else" can find relatives or friends to live with for a short time when faced with the alternative of paying for foster care.

We live in a society of money, and it is a fact of American life that anything worthwhile costs money. Toward this end, it is strongly urged that even those agencies that are completely financed by local, state, or federal tax funds, explore the possibility of charging abusive parents or adults for services rendered on an ability-to-pay basis. This payment should result from a mutual or court-ordered agreement, should include the abuser in the decision of how much to pay, and should be enforceable.

Foster Care

We must reevaluate the wisdom of foster care for children and consider the alternative of removing the abuser whenever possible. Foster care is extremely expensive, not only in terms of dollars but also in terms of the children's emotional well-being. Single placements of abused children are a rarity, and foster care often becomes an end in itself. Perhaps the abuser can be removed temporarily during the day, for the evening, or for whatever time is indicated. This alternative demands ingenuity, skill, and initiative and is much more difficult to accomplish than simply removing a child who has no say in the matter. Yet in the long run, for the sake of all concerned, it is best.

In some circumstances there is a demonstrable need for foster care. On these occasions foster care should be used prudently and with therapeutic goals for the child and the adult(s) in mind. It should be used as a last resort in abuse rather than the first. When it is used to accomplish certain goals, the reason(s) for placement should be clearly stated in writing to the parents, other agencies, and —yes—the child.

Rights of the Child

We must reevaluate the role of children and give priority to them. For too long we have treated the abused child as inferior to the adult abuser. The rights and wishes of the parent have taken precedence over those of the child, and in any accusation that is unsubstantiated, the child has had to prove the abuse.

Children who have been abused are frequently placed in foster care while the abusive adult remains in the home. This practice is analogous to locking up the victim of the crime and permitting the criminal to remain in the community. Instead of the "knee-jerk" response of placing the child in foster care, some thought should be given to removing *the abuser* from the home. This can be done in many instances by casework, court order, or an appeal, but it must be followed by immediate service to the abuser and the family to reunite them as soon as practicable.

In sexual abuse, particularly, we must stop harassing female victims by insisting on vaginal examinations and polygraph tests. Most of the time an examination of the penis of the suspected abuser would show as much as a vaginal examination—nothing.

Agency policy and practices must recognize children as individuals. They should be given separate appointments to be seen individually and apart from their parents (this includes mailing them confirmations of their appointments if they are old enough to read); the office should be a comfortable setting for children as well as adults; and their permission should be asked for such actions as contacting teachers.

Legal Representation

Attorneys serve a separate, valuable function for the adult, the child, and the agency. Adults should not be favored at the expense of an abused child; neither should they be inferior. Legally, each needs representation to insure his or her constitutional rights. The prevailing attitude has been that attorneys are inimical to the welfare of the abused child if they are retained by abusive parents. Conversely, they are viewed as valuable allies and members of the "treatment team" if they are in the employ of the agency. A variation on this attitude is that the opposing attorney "deals with technicalities and cares nothing about the child," while the agency attorney is "first committed to the welfare of the child but within the framework of the law." Inferentially the welfare of the child is always associated with the agency, specifically with the professional within the agency being challenged.

We should offer training to social workers, psychologists, and others in the behavioral sciences to acquaint them with legal processes. As a very practical alternative, professionals involved in child abuse might well ask local bar associations to work with them.

Referral

It is not true that referral of difficult cases (a) shifts the legal responsibility to another agency or person, (b) means that referred cases will be seen, and (c) insures that the clients will be treated and will become nonabusive. Referral must be recognized as having many variations, depending on to whom the abusers are referred, the attitude of the agency toward abusers, the competence of its professionals, their workload, and many other factors.

Rarely, if ever, can an agency legally charged with treating abusers and protecting abused children shift its legal responsibility to another. Consultation is a viable and worthwhile alternative to referring out abuse cases. In this sense, we might think of "referral in" rather than "referral out." Instead of merely telling abusers that they are being referred elsewhere, when referral is absolutely necessary, a written agreement should be drawn up between the agencies, the adults, and the children involved, outlining the responsibilities of all concerned.

Self-Help Groups

Self-help groups of abusers can be viable alternatives to agency or professional treatment. Many professionals give grudging respect to such self-help groups as Alcoholics Anonymous, Recovery, Inc., and Gamblers Anonymous yet do not accept them as legitimate approaches to the problems, probably because these groups do not use the same treatment model as the professional criticizing the group. Exactly the same is true of Parents Anonymous, which has a membership of self-identified abusers, many of whom have been labeled as "abusive."

Self-help groups are effective or ineffective to the extent that individuals involve themselves. The failure of one abuser to profit from such a group should no more be "held against" Parents Anonymous than the failure of one patient to respond to therapeutic effort should be held against the therapist. We must recognize that there are many routes to the same destination, and some prefer one over another. Just as some professionals have seen abusers who claim that they did not profit from Parents Anonymous, it is probably true that a majority of the membership of Parents Anonymous have not profited from professional effort.

Parents Anonymous received a grant of nearly $200,000 in July 1974 to assist in developing a nationwide program. It is hoped that the growth of this organization will be welcomed rather than resisted by professionals.

Termination of Cases

Current policy holds that abuse cases need not be terminated or closed out unless the child and the family leave the agency's jurisdiction and that closure will be determined by observation of the home situation and self-report of the parent or adult abuser. But cases can be closed if we establish short-range goals and measurable criteria for closure.

This final, and perhaps most important, factor in developing an economical, efficient, streamlined approach and new strategy rests with the so-called abusers themselves. Treatment is a contractual process between the professional, the child, and the adult(s) involved. The short-range goal in abuse cases is fundamental—no more abuse. Meeting the physical and psychological needs of the child and the adults might be the long-range goal. A realistic criterion for closure might well be a mutually agreed upon length of time without a recurrence of abuse or the factors that led to the abuse.

Is there a need for change? Can change occur? What is needed? What are the barriers?

Is there a need for change? Yes. Change is needed on all fronts: philosophical, theoretical, and practical. Child abuse is the direct result of our attitudes toward children and toward child rearing. Child abuse is the result of inadequate laws protecting children and of laws that favor the abuser rather than the abused. In only a very small percentage of cases is child abuse a symptom of mental illness or mental instability; those cases should not be treated within the framework of existing mental health programs and in the belief that everyone is pathological or disturbed. Change is needed in treatment of abuse. Currently, our national effort must be described as non-treatment of abuse.

Can change occur? The answer is yes, if America is willing to make a serious national commitment to the reduction of child abuse. This will require efforts on many fronts, of which treatment is but one. Education and alternative child-rearing practices must be imbued in the fabric of the people. Children must be liberated and be given the dignity, along with the constitutional guarantees, of all Americans. Those interested in the problem must develop a discipline and effort separate and apart from existing philosophies. This growth and development can only occur through basic research, innovative ideas based on the view that child abuse is a separate entity, and university-level training of specialists in the field.

We must enact laws that give children equal protection. While this seems rather mild, it is basic. We must guarantee them the right to life once they are born, for only with legal protection and guarantees can we *prevent* child abuse.

Philosophically, we must also reassess our notions about treatment and the treatment process. Professionals must relate to abusers as humans, and abusers must be given the opportunity of relating to individuals who may be able to assist them. Professionals in the field must rediscover humanity. Only through recognition that most of the abusers in America are quite normal in all respects save child rearing will we make significant progress. Coupled with the realization that professionals are not superior and abusers are not inferior must be acceptance of the idea that the abusive parent or adult is not superior to the abused child.

The barriers to change are many. First and foremost will be the reluctance of established and entrenched interests in private and public agencies to reject as unworkable a philosophy that is demonstrably inefficient, costly, and of limited value. Second, resistance will be found among professionals who are comfortable within a framework that views the persons experiencing difficulty as inferior to them. Current practices reinforce the authoritarian needs of professionals but do little to treat abuse. Third, a measure of resistance can be expected from some clergy and many among the general public.

In a real sense, change is inevitable, for how much longer will our national conscience tolerate the systematic disenfranchisement of a group of Americans, many of whom are treated worse than animals? It is enlightening to observe the rapidity with which federal employees and members of Congress recently moved to abolish the practice of "soring" Tennessee Walking Horses. With the same concern and commitment, America may move legislatively, emotionally, and reasonably to protect the very existence of some children.

Throughout this discussion we have seen that the treatment of abuse has been assigned to agencies that function under a quasi-therapeutic, historical system. Nationwide, current efforts to meet the problem and treat the children and adults involved are largely unsuccessful. One alternative is to establish another system, which is not burdened by historical antecedents that make treatment all but impossible. That is unnecessary. Within the existing agencies and system we have the necessary intellectual and human capabilities. What we need are flexibility, imagination, and initiative combined with information about child abuse.

CHAPTER SIX

General Treatment of the Physical Abuser

Problems in Handling Abuse Cases

There are several common, practical problems encountered in most abuse cases, physical or sexual. Among them are: how to contact the abuser after receiving the complaint; the abuser's resistance, denial, and hostility; and seduction of the therapist. It is not uncommon for inexperienced workers and therapists to become so anxious and defensive in the initial contact(s) with their clients that no meaningful relationships are established and no services are offered. Many of these problems can be alleviated through experience and good supervision. Let us discuss some of them before going on to an overall view of treatment, group treatment, and the treatment aspects of each type of abuser presented in the typology.

Generally, the laws of each state define abuse, mandate the reporting procedures, and designate agencies to receive abuse complaints. In the usual chain of events in a public agency, the complaint is received by an intake worker and through channels it is given to a general service worker or specialized protective service worker. After contact and evaluation, the professional then insures the protection of the child and often must report his or her findings to a court of appropriate jurisdiction.

At the outset, it is important to keep in mind several factors: Society has a legal right to protect children, and this right is invested in the professional, who, at first contact with the situation, becomes the legal representative of the state. The professional fulfills the sometimes contradictory functions of offering treatment while at the same time serving as an arm of the criminal justice system. Sometimes professionals must decide whether to refer a case to court. This raises ethical questions, and the known or suspected abuser should be notified that what he or she says to the investigator may contribute to a decision to prosecute.

After the complaint is received and assigned, contact should be made as soon as possible, within an hour of the time the complaint is received. The information available and the circumstances of the complaint will determine who will be seen first, the child or the adult(s). Clearly, the prosecutive function of the state is immediately concerned with the health or welfare of the child, and the right of the state transcends that of the parent in this instance. Further, as a representative of society, the professional does have the right (or should have if it is not clearly stated in the law) to contact the child at any time or place for the initial investigation of the complaint. If necessary, the child may be seen at a hospital, in the home, or at school.

The greatest stumbling block for the beginner is the initial visit. The inexperienced professional often feels like (and truly is) an intruder. He or she is defensive, uncomfortable in acting with authority, does not wish to discuss the complaint, and usually expects far too much from the initial contact and investigation. The goals of first contact are very limited and should consist of:

Telling the suspected abuser why the professional is there (i.e., an abuse complaint), the authority by which the professional is there, the agency involved, and the professional's name.

Seeing the child and insuring that medical treatment is given if indicated. If the child's physical well-being seems to be in jeopardy, the abuser should be removed or the child should be moved temporarily.

An appointment should be made for an office interview the following day.

Resistance and denial usually occur at first contact; this is a positive rather than a negative clinical sign. It means the suspected or real abuser is in contact with reality or at least has knowledge of the negative connotation of abuse, and it shows strength in the individual that can later be used positively in therapy.

Some problems frequently encountered with abusive adults are:

1. *Hostility in Males.* Generally this is a means that males in our society learn in order to control others, particularly females. It is a normal response and to be expected. After all, if *you* were accused of harming or abusing your child, wouldn't you be hostile?

The most ineffective manner of handling hostility is for the professional also to become hostile and authoritarian, for then the therapist has agreed to "play the abuser's game." There are several ways of coping with this hostility; one of the most effective is to give a human response such as, "I can see how you would be angry." At initial contact, one should also remember that the investigator did not cause the anger but is there as a result of the reported person's behavior.

2. *Crying in Females.* Just as males learn to use anger, many females control people by crying. The same advice given above applies to the female who cries. The best manner of handling this situation is to keep her talking.

3. *Denial of Abuse.* This is to be expected on initial contact. The professional should always be listening, for many times even as the patient is denying abuse, he or she will be offering an explanation that is so implausible that it is in effect an admission. Admission is not a necessity for treatment.

4. *Concern over "Who reported me?"* This mechanism is employed to divert attention from the child and the alleged abuser to some other person. Inexperienced persons often become defensive and state, "I'm sorry, but by law I cannot tell you." This reply adds legitimacy to the argument, and permits the alleged abuser to embark upon a thirty-minute tirade interpreting the Constitution of the United States. Usually, the "right to face one's accuser" is the first argument, followed by everything except the Eighteenth and Twenty-first Amendments to the Constitution. The professional should handle this problem by redirecting the focus to the child, the alleged

abuser, and the immediate situation. In almost all abuse cases the alleged abuser knows exactly who turned in the report.

After the initial contact, there is frequently a drawing together of the immediate and extended family. Sometimes the alleged abuser will appear with grandmother, grandfather, uncles, aunts, cousins, and a minister in tow, all of whom wish to discuss the complaint. The only realistic way to handle this situation is to see them all individually but to give priority to seeing the suspected abuser. The others can be interviewed later.

5. *Verbal Seduction.* At its most obvious, people will try to give interpersonal signals to therapists of the opposite sex and attempt to deal with them as members of the opposite sex. Another ploy, with members of the same sex, is to explore similarities in personal background, such as marriage, schooling, children, and military service.

Verbal seduction should be recognized as an early attempt to establish a relationship, a way to avoid discussing the abuse, and a means of "handling" the therapist. In working with verbal seduction, the therapist should remember that the assignment was not made on the basis of the professional's reproductive capacity or sexual identification, schooling, or military background, but because he or she is capable of providing professional service.

6. *Verbal Attack.* This defense is related to the previous ploy and is used to arouse anxiety in the therapist. It can take the form of "You are too young" or "too old"; "A man can't understand a woman's problems" or "A woman can't understand a man's problems"; "You are less (or more) educated than I am," and so on. There is really no need for this type of sparring and interaction. The professional is employed by the agency to deal with the complaint and should do exactly that.

7. *Appearance of an Attorney.* Agencies and professionals have been bludgeoned over and over again by attorneys, and many find that the home from which the child was removed "isn't so bad after all" once an attorney enters the picture. Agency beginners who feel safe, secure, and knowledgeable with their state university training and sharp wits need only wait until their first court case and an attorney's cross-examination. The newly minted public agency em-

ployee dealing with child abuse might apply that rapierlike mind to generating responses to some of the following commonly asked questions by attorneys: "Would you be kind enough to enlighten the court as to how your major in Shakespearean Literature and minor in Oceanography qualify you as an expert on child abuse?" "If you have no children of your own, would you tell us what qualifies you as an expert on raising children?" (For heaven's sake, don't say, "Because I studied it a lot in the university.") "You say you have children of your own. Have you ever spanked them or sworn at them?"

Every agency needs legal counsel not to protect the feelings of its professionals but for the protection of the children. No professional should ever appear in court without an attorney. Attorneys for parents serve a very real and worthwhile service, for parents have rights and should be represented by counsel. But so does the child need an attorney!

It has been suggested that agency administrators contact the nearest law school in their state and arrange for their staff to be cross-examined by third-year law students. This interrogation in a mock court proceeding should be severe and in depth. Afterwards the professional and the interrogating law student could be seated together at lunch to review their interaction.

Professionals need to be taught how to be good witnesses and to understand the lawyer's role, purpose, and direction. This behavior is easily learned, and there is great advantage in acquiring it in a setting other than actual court proceedings.

8. *Unwanted Intervention.* This problem is one that should be handled by administrators but is often overlooked. As an abuse case becomes well known (particularly a case of sexual abuse), a whole host of persons want to become involved. Unthinking but curious "professionals" such as school counselors, shelter personnel, detectives, and foster parents will sometimes call very young children in to discuss the abuse in detail. On being confronted their response is usually, "I told her she didn't have to discuss it with me but she wanted to." The adult may be technically correct, but has managed to coerce the child into discussing the matter. Other unwanted intervenors are ministers, relatives, and friends.

Children who are abused should be told that they are not to discuss the event with anyone other than the therapist, not because it was "bad" or "dirty" but because it is necessary to talk to one person and only to one. With very young children one can explain this by saying, "It's just like your doctor. You only go to one who cares about you and only talk with that one. You don't go to several doctors unless your doctor asks you to see another one." They can usually accept this interpretation.

Agency administrators should take a more active role in insuring that the children in their care are assigned to a therapist and are protected from unwanted intervention. In the event of repeated violations and inquisitiveness by outsiders, the administrator should talk to the offending party, and if that does not put an end to the questioning, to that person's superior. If necessary the intervenor's professional organization or licensing unit should be notified in writing.

Needless to say, the professional in charge of the abuse case should never discuss it except for professional reasons such as consultation or supervision. The case should not be discussed with one's coworkers, spouse, or friends, or at cocktail parties. A professional who does discuss confidential matters with others should be discharged from his or her position.

9. *Relationships with Other Agencies.* This matter is a crucial one in child abuse because the protection of the child is at stake. There should be one central telephone number for abuse cases that a hospital, the police, a mental health agency, a family service agency, or a school can call. They should not have to seek out Mr. Jones, "who is assigned to abuse cases." If Mr. Jones is sick, on vacation, or busy on another case, the caller should be referred to someone who can handle the call immediately, any time of the day or night. It is the *agency* that should be called, not an *individual* within the agency.

Relationships with the police need special consideration and attention. Police officers are in the community twenty-four hours a day, know the community well, and are in contact with possible abuse situations. But they are also pressed for time and simply cannot spend a half an hour tracking down a professional to report something that merits attention and then have to make out a written report. The solution to police–abuse agency relationships in one city was quite simple. A protective service worker would call the officer and ask for the information. Not too surprisingly, when the police suspected abuse they would call the agency since they could be sure they would not have to type out lengthy reports.

When hospitals call about suspected abuse, a professional should go to the hospital immediately. Hospital personnel and physicians are busy people and cannot wait for Monday morning if abuse occurs Friday night. There are also therapeutic implications. If the abused child is to be photographed (a Polaroid color camera is advisable), it is much better to have a sensitive professional take the pictures than a rushed, overburdened detective.

10. *Relationships with News Media.* This important problem is often overlooked. Many agencies have had difficulties because they take the position that some matters of public record are confidential. Others have routinely asked reporters not to publicize *any* case on the grounds that it may be injurious to the child, the parents, the community, or the agency. This position is unrealistic and one with which news personnel cannot abide.

News is news and will be reported. Reporters are not insensitive to children and will not publish certain stories if the request is legitimate. But they would be failing in their jobs if they did not report any cases. Some agency administrators and personnel have even tried to dictate how a story should be written in order to protect the agency at all costs (even when an error has occurred). This is ludicrous, rather like a reporter's telling a therapist how to handle a particular case—that is something that is never done, it should be added.

As in therapy with patients, honesty is not the best policy—it is the only policy. This is particularly true with investigative reporters, as some agency administrators have learned when a child is killed by an abuser with whom the agency should have been working. Death is newsworthy, death by assault particularly so, and when it involves a child it rates even more attention. The agency should provide the "who, what, why, when, where, and how," honestly and promptly. This is not the time to issue self-serving statements, for they will immediately be recognized for what they are. One final word of advice: Do not argue with a newspaper unless you own one!

11. *Public Education.* There is little if any public education in connection with physical or sexual abuse of children. What little is given is not offered by professionals in the field but by the news media. Some of it is downright misleading. For example, one agency administrator stressed police patrol around elementary schools to prevent sexual abuse. This is a popular and "safe" approach, but in this instance the administrator knew full well the realities of sexual abuse—most of it is perpetrated by relatives and adults known to the child. He defended his statement by saying, "With publicity, we can obtain much-needed personnel."

Public education sometimes implies that administrators must take an unpopular stand for the moment in order to secure long-range benefits. It implies active involvement with educational programs and truthful assessments of an agency's capabilities and limitations. The public will accept the agency's deficiencies and try to assist in overcoming them, but it will not stand for misleading and hypocritical statements.

General Treatment Principles

The best indicator of future behavior is past behavior. Without some sort of intervention the physical abuser will continue to harm a child. If effective intervention (or we may call it "treatment") is offered, abuse can and will cease. Treatment involves working with the adult and child toward the primary goal of nonabusive behavior. This cannot be accomplished by dictating lengthy reports, consulting, or referring. These measures, while frequently both necessary and desirable from an agency point of view, do nothing to diagnose, treat, or resolve the situation.

The primary effort must be directed in a treatment relationship. A therapeutic and treatment-oriented relationship is necessary if abusers are to be helped. A therapeutic relationship involves goals, the primary one being nonabuse; a give-and-take between the professional and the patient; and consistency. In contrast, in many state and county public agencies, professionals are encouraged not to invest any feeling in abusers. There must be a professional assessment of the type of abuse and the parent-child interaction that results in abusive behavior. |

Abuse can best be understood in terms of the *family triad;* in its simplest form it consists of adult male, adult female, and child. A simple drawing illustrates the lines of interaction in the triad and shows that each party is vitally involved in the abuse situation. That

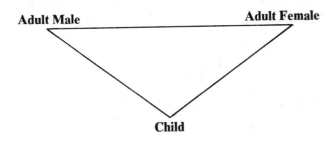

does not mean that physical abuse by one parent has the overt agreement of the other, or of the child, nor does it imply that abuse cannot occur without the conscious knowledge of all. It does mean, however, that all three must receive some professional treatment if the abuse is to be resolved.

One parent may deny having knowledge of the other's abuse, but as the relationship with the therapist develops, it is not uncommon later for the "unknowing parent" to admit knowledge or at least a sense of awareness. This aspect has a practical application. Many times when a stepparent abuses a child or children of the natural parent, the latter will terminate the marriage. In this sense, parents have a choice, and that choice is not to permit the abuse of their children.

Professionals should be aware of the triad in abuse cases for it bears on treatment strategy in a number of ways:

All three members are involved and each one needs professional intervention in treating the abuse. To illustrate, the author worked with a physically abusive father and directed all efforts toward him. When the father stopped abusing, the mother began to goad him until he again mistreated the children. Finally, when he ceased abusing the children entirely the marriage deteriorated and ended in divorce. The mother remarried, and predictably, the stepfather became abusive. For the beginning professional in abuse, it may be helpful to remember the analogous case of the alcoholic husband. Sometimes when he stops drinking there is a divorce, and it is not unheard of for the wife to marry another man with alcoholic tendencies. A patient who had ceased hitting his children clarified this matter in a very succinct way by stating, "My wife just can't stand prosperity!"

Some children who have been abused also cannot "stand prosperity." Conditioned to certain parental responses, they often go through lengthy "testing" to see if the change in parental behavior is real and permanent. Further, the children are psychologically comfortable in known and predictable patterns and often confuse non-abusive behavior in adults as a lack of limits. All children need and desire limits on their behavior as assurances of parental love and concern, and they too must go through a period of reeducation.

Abusers cannot be treated by "osmosis" or through another member of the triad. While this point should be self-evident, it is not to many professionals. Young female professionals are frequently afraid of older men and feel more comfortable working with the adult female to the exclusion of the threatening adult male. Similarly, many young male professionals feel uncomfortable and inadequate dealing with older women, and consequently they focus on the adult male. Finally, there are some professionals who are threatened by adults and focus only on the child. All of them delude themselves into thinking they are effectuating basic personality changes in the persons in the triad not being seen through their efforts with the one with whom they feel comfortable.

This difficulty is important to the supervisory, treatment, and planning aspects of each case. Each member of the triad must be seen professionally and in a therapeutic relationship. If professionals are unwilling or unable to deal with one person in the triad this fact should be recognized not as a limitation but as a reality. This is one of the many reasons why it is often wise to assign more than one worker to the same abuse case.

Secondary effort may involve environmental, financial, voca-

tional, marriage, or other counseling. While our primary problem is adult behavior that is injurious to children, other factors may contribute to an adult's becoming abusive. However, the focus of the therapy should not shift to peripheral or contributory factors. This is not to say that we should not be attuned to stresses and strains affecting the triad that can contribute to abusive behavior. In the vast majority of cases, however, they are secondary factors.

Separate triads exist in multi-children families. Professionals sometimes overlook the fact that each child in the family has a separate and distinct personality and a different set of relationships with the adults. For this reason, it is extremely important to develop a therapeutic relationship with each child. Further, the therapist will note that different children move at different speeds, articulate different perceptions and concerns, and display different affective patterns. In many instances, it is advisable for one therapist to assume responsibility for the adults in a triad, and another for the children. This is too "expensive" for most agencies but is highly desirable.

Treatment Strategy

Each type of physical abuser presents a different set of problems in need of resolution or treatment. First and foremost in every case we should have, as our primary goal, *nonabusive behavior.* That is to say, we must focus on the abuse of the parents and work with them toward developing ways of dealing with their children that do not harm them physically. The development of insight or ventilation of feeling are important only if the abuser ceases abusing. In the vast majority of cases, when parents cease using physical means to control their children's behavior, they will find ways that are destructive to a child through the use of words. The secondary goal then is open communication with the children.

There are three steps in achieving the primary goal of nonabusive behavior:

1. Identification of parental stress.
2. Identification of which behavior by the children will irritate

or enrage the adult, resulting in physical abuse.

    3. Development of alternative coping mechanisms.

Most of us know when we are irritated or vulnerable to aggression. Some people do not wish to be approached on any matter upon arising in the morning or not until after the "second cup of coffee." Others are vulnerable upon returning home at night from work or immediately after dinner. Still others have low levels of tolerance during weekends, and some are under duress from the constant pressures of a child in the home twenty-four hours a day. Most parents and most children sense and identify stress-provoking situations, but most abusive parents do not. Further, their children do not learn to approach Mom or Dad at given times. With discussion, parents can be helped to identify those times when they are most likely to aggress and to communicate this to their children.

Many abusive parents feel that they are supposed to love their child at all times, to react appropriately (i.e. with constant acceptance of the child's behavior), and never to admit anger. Then when they abuse they become guilt-ridden and angry with themselves. This, in turn, is directed against the child and results in a never-ending circle of abuse. Abusive parents have to be helped to accept that all parents are "down" at certain times and that all parents become angry at times. Further, they must be helped to accept that at times *they have a right to be angry*. With the recognition and acceptance of these facts, abusive parents begin to view themselves as not too different from other parents, and in many instances they experience a dramatic increase in self-image, self-confidence, and self-acceptance.

Some abusive parents will state that they do not know when they are vulnerable or likely to become irritated with their children. A rather simple technique is to have them keep a diary (if they can write) about how they feel each hour from arising until bedtime. Sometimes it is also helpful to have them note how they feel when the children leave home for school, during the children's naps, in the evening, etc. For those who are employed, it sometimes seems quite helpful to have them write down their reactions during the period when they are at work, as well as how they feel at home. Having identified the time when the parent or adult caretaker is likely to be irritated, we should tell him or her to be aware each day of those vulnerable hours and to tell the children to choose other times to approach the parent.

To identify which behavior will cause anger in the adult is sometimes difficult. Some parents will say that their children are "bad at all times" or that the children are "fussy" or "whiney," but it is necessary to pin down specific behavior or a sequence of behavior. In infants and young children crying seems to arouse anxiety and/or anger in many parents. So, too, does rebellious behavior, such as going out in the street or getting into the cupboards, and "defiant" behavior, such as the child's automatically saying no to any request.

Probably the greatest area of conflict between parent and child is toilet training. Actually, if one takes an objective view of the matter, other than for convenience, there is really no need to toilet train a child before it goes to school. Yet for many parents, there is a status factor connected with toilet training. In some circles (and it is not restricted to any class, race, or income category), it is fashionable to toilet train children as soon as possible. One mother who abused her child proudly told the author that she had "completely toilet trained John [her son] at nine months." Her neighbors were quite in awe of this feat, and she was somewhat let down when she was told, "You haven't really toilet trained John, you are simply very adept at catching him at the right time!"

Children seem to sense parental concern over toilet training and react accordingly. It is one behavior in which the child can control the parent, express love or anger, and receive immediate reinforcement. It is amazing how many mothers sit by their children with furrowed brows awaiting the delivery of urine or feces. It is more amazing to see how quickly the children pick up the mother's or father's anxiety and withhold defecation and urination until exactly four minutes after they are removed from the potty seat. This behavior causes prolonged bathroom sessions, anxiety, anger, and abuse.

The key point is that adult abusers be specific about the behavior that disturbs them, even if it seems to be a continuous sequence of behavior. Another variable that is important is whether the child's behavior is irritating all the time or part of the time. If a parent states that crying causes anger, it is necessary to find out if it always has that effect or if he or she only becomes angry some of the time.

The third step is to develop alternative coping mechanisms. Have the parents explore and try out nonphysical methods. If some coping mechanisms have failed, the therapist can offer ten or fifteen other nonabusive means of handling behavior. These alternative coping mechanisms can then be tried, and if they are unsuccessful, ten more can be suggested. Take the hypothetical case of an abusive mother who cannot tolerate her infant's crying:

Mother states that she cannot stand the baby crying at any time of the day or night. At this point it is not important whether she cried a lot when she was a baby, whether crying arouses anxiety, or whether it reminds her of anything; the baby's crying results in severe physical abuse. The mother simply relates that the incessant crying angers her. We then ask how she has attempted to cope with the crying, and she gets so upset she does nothing until she hits the infant. We then offer her alternative coping mechanisms, which are nonabusive in nature. Some obvious ones are:

1. Check for an unfastened pin (this is never the case!).
2. Rock the baby.
3. Sing to the baby.
4. Give the baby a bottle.
5. See if the diaper needs changing.
6. Turn up the radio.
7. Leave the room.
8. Distract the baby with a moving object, such as a toy.
9. Involve another human with the baby, a sibling or another adult.

All these mechanisms involve the mother in a positive or negative action that protects both her and the baby. At this point it does not matter whether the selection is the best for the baby in the long run. The fact is, it is not being battered.

Let us now assume that the mother tries each of these mechanisms and none work for her. We then develop another set of nonabusive actions. We must remember that the mother is trying alternatives to battering the child. We might recommend:

10. Call a neighbor and ask if she can determine the cause.

11. Take the infant to a well-baby clinic, a physician, or other medical resource if finances permit.

12. Turn the baby from its back to its stomach, or vice versa.

13. Place the baby where it can hear the television, the radio, or other voices.

14. Vacuum another room.

15. Talk to the baby.

16. See if the room is too hot or too cold.

17. Shut the door to baby's room and watch television.

18. Leave the house temporarily.

Again we might question the wisdom of some of these measures, but they have one thing in comon: None involve striking the child. All suggest ways of meeting either the child's needs or the mother's, and none are abusive.

Children's crying is a relatively simple behavior to deal with. Others are more complex and difficult, and the problem is compounded by the fact that the parent is conditioned to hitting the child and lacks a repertoire of alternatives. This strategy and technique is effective only to the degree that parents or adult abusers are assisted by the therapist in defining specific behavior. It is not uncommon in the beginning for abusive adults to offer very broad, general, and undefinable problems presented by the children. Complaints of the child's being "demanding," "irritable," "mean," and "disrespectful" are indicative of feelings about the child but are not specific enough to work with in this technique.

Working with Adult Abusers in Groups

In a one-to-one relationship the burden is theoretically on both the adult abuser and the therapist to generate nonphysical means of coping with children. But the task of developing alternatives can be extremely difficult, and the burden usually falls on the therapist. If the alternatives are not effective, the fault lies with the therapist. As any therapist well knows, offering solutions for a patient's problems is fraught with difficulty or danger. For these reasons, as well as for efficiency and economy, groups seem to be extremely effective.

Obviously, one does not start a group by informing abusive parents that " a group of abusers is being started, and would you like to join?" Rather, adult abusers and their spouses are approached individually on the basis that *all* parents have problems with their children and that perhaps by discussing the stress parents and children experience, children's behavior, and methods of coping with it, they can become more effective parents. This approach removes any accusation of blame or fault, has a certain amount of appeal to many abusive adults who often have no contacts outside the home, and permits them to work directly on the problem. In fact, it is not even necessary that parents be abusive to profit from this technique. It is important that the therapist does not pressure them into joining and that the adults know that they will also have a continuing professional relationship with a therapist on an individual basis.

Mechanics of Initiating the First Meeting. After a sufficient number of parents have agreed to join the group it is necessary to find a time to meet. Meetings should last about 90 minutes. The easiest way is to ask the parents to "block out" times they would prefer to meet on a standard monthly form, indicating their first, second, and third choices. Jobs and other commitments will make it impossible for some people to meet when the others wish. For this reason, it is wise to begin with a sizable number of parents and perhaps start two groups.

After finding a time when eight to twelve parents can meet, the therapist should arrange the date of the first meeting and inform each person in the group of the time and place. The therapist should arrange for the first meeting place, but should tell the parents that if they wish, they may meet elsewhere in the future.

In scheduling the first meeting, the therapist should look for a central location, check with the parents about arranging for baby-sitters if the children are not in foster care, and discuss transportation problems. Children should not be left unattended in order for parents to attend meetings, and this can be stressed as a first step in developing appropriate child-care mechanisms. The parents can usually find baby-sitters; the therapist should discuss the situation with those who state they are unable to find anyone to watch their children, as this may be a form of resistance. As a last resort, the therapist may wish to arrange for volunteers to baby-sit or provide transportation. After the first meeting or during the latter part of the first one, the parents may wish to discuss these matters with the group. It is not unusual at this point for abusers to use transportation difficulties or the lack of baby-sitters to express dependency needs, resistance, and, sometimes anger.

At the first meeting, the role of the therapist should be to put everyone at ease and reduce the level of anxiety. For many abusive adults, attendance at the first meeting is a milestone in itself. Many have no friends, rarely leave the home, and will bring quite a lot of anxiety with them. Before the meeting the therapist should have discussed individually with the adults the matter of names. Some will feel uncomfortable and will insist on anonymity. Others will have no hesitation in stating their names. The wishes of each should be respected. Normally the therapist will start the meeting by introducing himself (herself) and telling a little about his or her interests and activities. This will set a pattern for the others, and they will then go around the circle stating their names, interests, children, and ages.

After these brief self-introductions, the therapist should offer some structure by saying: "You all know me individually and I know you. A number of you have said you wanted to become more effective parents. All of us have trouble or difficulty in bringing up children. This is normal. By getting together, we all hope to be better able to deal with our children." The therapist should then explain that the purpose of the discussions will be (1) to identify when parents are under stress, (2) to identify children's behavior that creates difficulties for the members of the group, and (3) to help one another find appropriate ways of handling their children. The group will find many commonalities in the situations in which they perceive themselves as tense, irritable, or otherwise nonreceptive to their children. In a short time, most of them will become comfortable and begin talking about their children's behavior.

When discussing behavior that perplexes or angers a parent, the therapist should center on one behavior and ask members of the group if they ever experienced the same behavior in their children and how they handled it. If they have not, they can suggest ways of coping with it.

It is advisable to have a blackboard or large sheets of paper on which the various alternative methods that are suggested can be listed for all to see. After 20 to 30 alternatives (to striking the child) have been written down the therapist can then ask the person who brought up the specific behavior if he or she would like to try some of them. At this point, particularly during the first few meetings of the group, the parent will probably respond that he or she had tried ten of these suggestions and "none worked." This is normal and to be expected. The therapist should then ask the parent to write down the remaining alternatives and try them if the behavior arises during the next week. The therapist can then move to another person and repeat the process.

Before the end of the first meeting, which should last ninety minutes, the therapist should review the purpose of the group, the accomplishments of the first meeting, and schedule the second meeting for the next week. Finally, the parents should be asked to observe their children closely during the following week and write down any irritating behavior and to monitor their own feelings to determine when they are vulnerable. Asking them to monitor themselves and their children and to write down their observations gives them "work" to do every day on their problems. Further, it keeps them aware that the resolution of their child-rearing patterns will not come from one session per week but from working every day on the matter.

A few days after the first meeting, it is often helpful for the therapist to call each patient (assuming of course that they have telephones) or to see each one briefly. They should be asked if they are monitoring themselves and their children and making a list. The phone contact need not be more than ten minutes, but it gives the group continued support.

Subsequent Meetings of the Group. It cannot be stressed too strongly that the group must focus on parental stress and specific behavior on the part of the children. Some parents would rather discuss unrelated matters, such as their own childhood feelings, financial problems, or in-law problems, partly to meet their own unfulfilled needs and partly to avoid the problem. However, if one of the group brings up the question of constant stress from a boss, an in-law, or financial problems, these matters can and should be dealt with by the group, but the main focus of the discussion must remain on behavior.

If the group brings up matters that meet the personal needs of the therapist, and the therapist reinforces the discussion, the group will rapidly change its focus and meet these expectations. Similarly, if the therapist introduces a matter he or she is particularly concerned with, the group can quickly change.

Pitfalls to Avoid in the Group:

1. Criticism of any suggested alternative coping mechanism unless it would injure the child.

2. Breach of confidentiality. At the first meeting it should be clearly stated that the matters discussed by the group should not be mentioned outside the meeting. When routine consultation is in process with another therapist, the group should know that it is occurring and why.

3. Change in roles. On occasion a member of the group will ask the therapist to explain something to a caseworker, psychiatrist, or in-law, in other words, to intervene on his or her behalf. This is unwise as it changes the whole structure of the therapeutic role in the group and, obviously, in the relationship with the individual involved.

4. Nonpayment of fees. Every group member should be paying at least a token amount for professional services rendered, whether

these services are offered by a private practitioner under purchase-of-services agreements or by a private or public agency. As has been noted earlier we live in a society where something that is free is usually of no value. Payment is essential even if it costs more to process the payment than it is worth. The matter should be discussed individually with the patient if he or she fails to pay the fee.

Continued Group Movement. After four to six weekly meetings the members of the group will have become more comfortable with child-rearing mechanisms that are not physically abusive. At this time, it is desirable (but not always necessary) to give the children the opportunity to discuss their feelings about changes in parental behavior with a caseworker or other professional. During this period it is common for children to test out new parental behavior by "acting out" behavior.

At the first few group meetings the therapist should not evaluate suggestions or measures employed other than to point out those that could be harmful or dangerous. In one group, a mother who used to whip her 3-year-old son offered the idea that she should not strike her child nor should anyone else strike a child. Rather, one should forcibly place the child's head under water in a toilet bowl! Intervention by the therapist was obviously indicated. In another instance, a father whose son often came home with things that did not belong to him came up with the idea that instead of beating him, as he had in the past, he would handcuff the son for eight hours in the garage if the behavior was repeated. Again, intervention by the thearpist was necessary. Generally, however, parents do not suggest abusive alternatives.

After a number of meetings, when the group has coalesced, the therapist should begin moving it toward an examination of the effect of the alternative coping mechanisms on the children. The focus should change from strictly nonphysically abusive patterns to techniques that affect the children's welfare. Name-calling, distracting a child, reprimanding, depriving of privileges, or ignoring the child all miss the basic component of children's behavior: They act out in order to meet unfulfilled needs. Responses that are not physically abusive but are nevertheless punitive can only stunt the child, induce more of the same adverse behavior, or result in the child's becoming hostile, feeling guilty, or creating a poor self-image.

The consideration of the quality of adult-child interaction is difficult for some abusers as it is not easy for them to recognize that children have needs and desire a measure of independence. Quality of interaction really means good two-way communication between the adult and the child. A rather primitive interaction, which recognizes both parties and their mutual needs, would be a mother's saying to a child, "You are tired, and so am I." It is far better than saying, "You are mean, aren't you?" which places the burden of the interaction on the child and does nothing to resolve the situation.

One father used this sentence verbatim with his daughter. She in turn said, "No I'm not tired, I'm mad!" This was the beginning of communications between the two, and the father remarked to the group, "I didn't know the kids knew how they felt!" When they are aware that children also have needs, many parents will honestly attempt to "psych out" their children and will begin to anticipate stress not only in themselves but also in their children and in life situations that can cause problems for them both.

It is important that we recognize that parents or other adult caretakers not only can cease physically abusing their children but also can, with help, learn to communicate very well with them. Unfortunately, many professionals tend to equate the label "abusive" with "hopeless," which most parents assuredly are not.

All of us like to be wanted and needed, and seeking approval from others is a common human experience. With support and encouragement by a therapist in discussing problems of child and self, even parents who have been abusive have been astonished to learn that rearing children can be a pleasurable experience.

This view, which is not unique to the author, represents a denial of the attitude that most abusive parents are helpless, hopeless, inadequate forever, or "sick." To be sure, there are many abusive parents who lack motivation to change. There are some who are mentally inadequate to the tasks of child rearing, and there are a few who are mentally ill. But to categorize abusive parents in this way is to ignore and denigrate those who are willing and capable of change.

This view also reflects a change in the traditional approach to child abuse, in which the therapist is the expert or "superior" and the patient is "inferior." It involves caring about people who have been reported for abusing children, accepting them and their children as equals in problem solving, and a willingness to give of one's time and self when the need arises.

How People Change

Perhaps it would be best to discuss how people do *not* change if they are classified as "abusive." They do not change as a result of threats by professionals to remove their children. They do not change as a result of police or detectives conveying their feelings of disgust or abhorrence. They do not change as a result of paternalistic or maternalistic lectures by physicians, caseworkers, or other professionals. Finally, they do not change as a result of prosecution that results in fines, probation, or imprisonment. In fact, most of these approaches aggravate the problem rather than reduce it, for the parents become only more angry, bitter, and frustrated and project the blame onto the abused child.

People change because other people care about them as persons without necessarily approving of their behavior. In lay terms, people change because of positive feelings toward another whether those feelings are based on a need for acceptance, friendship, or love.

Most heavy smokers watch television ads and know that continued smoking can lead only to heart disease, an increased probability of cancer, and other disabilities. These ads (which really reinforce the nonsmokers' behavior rather than alter the smokers' behavior) cause many smokers to become anxious and to increase their cigarette consumption! But let a smoker be faced with a child who says, "Dad, why are you killing yourself? I love you and want you alive, not dead." The effect of this interaction has many times resulted in a cessation or drastic reduction of smoking. This change in behavior is not motivated by fear of the consequences of smoking but by love.

This point has many implications in the treatment of abusive parents. Child abuse is not comparable to most criminal offenses, for most of it is not wilful torture or harm for the sake of causing harm. Instead, it is a pattern of child rearing that for the most part is a learned behavior, integrated into other behavior and attitudinal patterns. In this respect it may be viewed as somewhat akin to the disease of alcoholism.

We may continue our treadmill of arrests, jail terms, and fines for alcoholics, but we are doing nothing about resolving alcoholism. By the same token, we may arrest, publicize, humiliate, and punish child abusers through legal processes, but we do nothing to resolve their problems. Those who feel that increased punishments, fines, or imprisonment will solve child abuse are punitive, naive, or simplistic —probably all three.

In fact, legal prosecution causes more problems for society. The child is often exposed to other caretakers during the term of imprisonment (relatives or a succession of foster homes); another adult enters the triad, and the relationships of the original one are disrupted; and in a few months or years the abuser is back home.

This is not to say that children do not need legal protection. In 8 to 15 percent of all physical abuse cases, society, through its courts, can and should move swiftly and expeditiously to terminate parental rights and place the children elsewhere permanently. Sad but true, this is particularly so with abusers with a long history of mental illness. But we really do not handle termination very well either. Usually, the judge places the child in foster care; no services are offered the parents; the parent retains an attorney, which act has the desired effect of frightening most agency administrators and personnel; the attorney asks for the return of the children after assurances by the parent; the judge relents; the children are returned to the home; and the cycle of abuse begins again.

The law alone cannot cope with the child abuser, nor can social sciences alone. It requires a close working relationship between the two, with legal protection of the child foremost *but* with treatment also offered to the abuser. This rarely occurs.

CHAPTER SEVEN

Treatment of Specific Types of Physical Abusers

The Socially and Parentally Incompetent Abuser

This type of abuser responds well to the group method, particularly if others in the same category are included in the group. With this type, we are faced with a learned behavior. That is, by contemporary child-care philosophy and standards, many of these parents would have been considered abused or harshly treated when they were youngsters.

One problem that should be dealt with in individual counseling rather than in the group is the feeling that many have of rejecting their parents along with the learned child abuse. Usually these abusers have strong positive feelings about their own parents and the rightness of their behavior and values. With assistance, they can be moved quite rapidly into accepting their parents as persons of worth but without continuing their abusive child-rearing practices.

This type of abuser is often faced with family and neighborhood pressures that reinforce abusive patterns. These factors must be minimized through the positive counterpressure of allegiance to and affiliation with the group.

There is no set way of assisting these abusers to deal with outside pressures to perpetuate the harsh, punitive treatment the patient and the patient's parents had to accept as children. On an individual basis, a change in child rearing to include nonabusive manners of dealing with behavior has been interpreted in different ways to different patients. In one instance, it was compared to the first child in an uneducated family who went on to college. In another, it was compared to the first member of the family who bought a house instead of renting. In still another, both the therapist and the patients worked toward minimizing contact with the extended family until new behavior patterns had become a way of life.

The children of this type of abuser also seem to require more help than do those whose parents fall into most of the other categories. This is probably due to the fact that the practices are part and parcel of a life style, or "family script," which is acted out generation after generation.

Resistance to new ideas and new behavior does not die easily. Many will question the efficiency of nonabusive techniques and will forecast a dim future for their children. Yet, when all is said and done, those in this category, probably more than any other, will become articulate zealots of nonabusive behavior once "converted." There is no common factor of social class, race, income, or religion among them, and their reactions to suggestions and the discussion vary. On the whole, though, they are articulate, have a normal native intelligence, and share a belief in "basic American values." The prognosis for this type of abuser is excellent.

The Frustrated and Displaced Abuser

Abusers in this category use projection as a defense mechanism, and projection of feelings onto children results in abuse. Out of this category has evolved the myth that all child abusers view children as objects rather than as people. That is true only of abusers of this type. Actually, they view all human beings, not just children, as objects when they project their anger onto others and assault them. Another distinction that should be made is that many of them view children as objects only during the period of abuse or assault. Many of them experience guilt feelings and a sense of wrongdoing over their abusive behavior, "but cannot help themselves."

The key to working with them is to develop other psychological mechanisms to handle their feelings. This does not imply in any sense that this type of abuser is mentally ill. Many people use projection as a defense mechanism, and place the blame for their own problems on others.

Some of the frustrated and displaced abusers seem to move quite rapidly into the use of denial as a temporary defense mechanism after involvement in a group. It is not uncommon for others to continue to use projection but to become selective in their choice of target after intervention. Usually the new target is a spouse (to a greater degree than before) or an animal. One mother who was horribly abusive to her daughter and would torture the child had a favored pet cat. Early in her group experience she ceased harming her child but targeted her once-loved cat. Eventually she was able to cope with frustration and express herself in a most controlled manner.

Another fairly common phenomenon after intervention is an inversion, a turning within of feelings, resulting in somatic complaints such as headaches, backaches, upset stomachs, loss of appetite, and difficulty in sleeping. Without medical foundation, a few have become semi-invalids upon cessation of child abuse. In a few instances, withdrawal becomes the defense mechanism. After discovery, report of abuse, and intervention (either in individual or group counseling), a few parents will become listless, sleep a lot, and become uninterested and apathetic.

Part of the treatment consists of helping the abusers to recognize the behavioral chain that results in abuse. That is, they must be assisted in identifying the frustrations that they experienced, for most have not, and be helped to recognize cognitively that an association exists between the frustration and the subsequent outbreak of anger. They must then be led to the realization that this anger is expressed toward the child rather than toward the source of frustration. Although they have accepted this explanation intellectually, it does not follow that they will accept it emotionally and act upon it. There is a continuing educational process of reviewing behavioral chains and pointing out the sequence of behavior. In time, the patient is helped to anticipate these chains, that is, to open "sensors" to see frustration looming, and then to decide how best to reduce the frustration without projection.

Some abusers in this type seem to "thrive on violence." It is not uncommon to find that if there are two adults in the home, they assault each other very frequently. It is difficult to know whether to classify these persons as Socially and Parentally Incompetent Abusers with a learned intergenerational persistence of violence, as Frustrated and Displaced Abusers, or as Subcultural Abusers. Perhaps it is a combination of the three, but nevertheless it is a reality. Violence done to each other seems to take on a quality of affirmation of their relationship or love. All of us know people who are never so much in love with their spouses as after a night of fighting!

Mr. and Mrs. H. lived in a public housing project. Mr. H. felt that his wife was "holding him back" from anything better than a cab driver's job. But she attributed their financial and housing problems to Mr. H.'s inadequacies, which she could "tick off" in detail and with rapidity.

Mr. H. was reported for continually hitting his three sons with a belt. After intervention, the couple decided not to assault each other or the children. After two months, the wife's chronic complaining and pointing out Mr. H.'s inadequacies "got to him." After leaving work at noon on Saturday, he had two bottles of beer. When he arrived home, he gave each of the children a small amount of money to go out to the play area of the housing project. Mrs. H. continued her complaining, and Mr. H. proceeded to beat her up. After the donnybrook, in the husband's words, "She was happy, I was happy, and the kids didn't see nothin'."

This illustration shows that the abuser can be selective in targeting, although the targeting behavior may be difficult to abandon. Another point that all therapists should consider is the reevaluation of therapeutic efforts. Generally, therapists are drawn from the middle class, and their treatment goal automatically becomes the abandonment of physical violence. This can be accomplished, but at what price to the family and children? If Mr. and Mrs. H. were to give up violence, in all likelihood they would get a divorce. The consequence of this type of therapy would be a broken home, all to meet the therapist's expectations of "proper" behavior.

In therapy with abusers we need to think of a "clinical trade-off." Our primary goal must remain constant, i.e., no abuse of children, but within this rule we can and should tolerate diverse solutions, some of which are contrary to middle-class values. In the case of Mr. and Mrs. H., the children are not physically abused (and three years after, at this writing, still have not been) but the parents do assault each other out of the presence of the children. In the view of the author, the tradeoff is acceptable.

The prognosis for the Frustrated and Displaced Abuser is good.

The Situational Abuser

Treatment of the situational abuser must be based on a careful examination by both the patient and the therapist of the factors that cause pressure, with a view toward reducing these pressures. This sometimes involves environmental manipulation, a divestment of responsibilities, if those responsibilities overwhelm the individual, and, in some instances, the use of homemaking, nursing, or other services.

Most situational abusers cannot see the forest for the trees in the sense that they are indeed overwhelmed, and may or may not know why, but see no immediate or long-term relief from their problems. Sometimes abuse is due to the entry of a stepparent on the scene (or the return of a parent who has been absent for a prolonged period of time due to employment or imprisonment). When someone interprets to the adults what is transpiring in the children, the parents become attuned to needs that had been overlooked. A sense of timing is needed. Children cannot adjust overnight to a new adult in the home, and much testing will occur. When the new adult realizes this, he or she will not feel the immediate need of asserting authority, knowing that in time the children will adjust.

An abuser of this type needs to set up a system of priorities of what things must be done, what things it would be nice to do, and what things are really unnecessary. Many place "a priority of one" on everything and thus become overwhelmed with the total demands.

The prognosis for the situational abuser is excellent.

The Neglectful Abuser

Max Wald of the State of Wisconsin, one of the greatest experts in the United States in the area of neglect, has stated that "probably the greatest decision an agency will make in neglect is the decision of whether or not to get involved *at all*." Although he was not speaking directly to the issue of the neglectful abuser, Wald took this position because once a neglect case is accepted, it is likely to remain with a public agency for years, even generations, and cost tens of thousands of dollars in direct aid and professional time with a very minimum return on society's investment.

The neglectful abuser uses a technique similar to one used by very young children: passive-aggressive behavior. The caseworker may visit, counsel, interview, lecture, plead, or whatever else he or she feels may effect a change; the client will agree (sometimes tearfully); and a day later the situation is the same. The homemaker instructs in homemaking skills and often becomes a house cleaner. Again, the client will agree to try harder, or do whatever the worker expects, only to ignore it, and in this manner the client expresses varying degrees of hostility.

Neglectful abusers are difficult to work with in a therapeutic setting. Although they can manage to go to town, to the local tavern, or to relatives in the adjoining state or county, they cannot keep an office appointment. It is erroneous to call them "unmotivated," a label that is frequently applied. They *are* motivated, but that motivation consists primarily of not having any more contact with authority figures than is absolutely necessary, and in this respect they are highly skilled and efficient. This passive, dependent, aggressive behavior can be seen in family planning. As one social worker complained to the author, "Sure you can get them to take the Pill when the school bus comes in the morning, but what do you do on Saturday and Sunday?"

Rather pessimistically, we must conclude that there are very few avenues for working with the person who neglects children to the point of endangering their lives. There are two obvious alternatives: "working around" the parents and trying to build in protection for the child by frequent visits by relatives, neighbors, caseworkers, homemakers, nurses, ministers, and others to check on the children; and placement of the children. The former appears to be the only realistic solution to the problem.

While it is more expensive in time, money, and effort to "work around" the parents, the alternative is less acceptable. Termination of parental rights, particularly in this category, is difficult. Furthermore, children who have experienced cultural, tactile, social, educational, and financial deprivation will not be the most adoptable. Finally, no court can or will order sterilization of a parent on these particular grounds, so more children will be born. Having children seems to give some merit and meaning to life, and some neglectful abusers might almost be considered "baby factories."

A final deficiency common to neglectful abusers is that most of them are nonverbal or have difficulty in communicating. This severely limits the treatment potential. This problem, combined with their fear of authority and their passive-aggressive behavior, makes them almost impossible to treat.

A sensitive, aware psychiatrist once remarked to the author, "Probably the best solution would be to create a housing sub-division next to a hospital with a public welfare agency right in the middle. In this manner society could insure to a degree the physical health and well-being of these youngsters." This idea is not at all far-fetched and perhaps should be explored in depth. It simply calls for Americans to recognize and accept the fact that some persons need continued care, and that for the sake of the children we should provide basic protections and guarantees of life. One may question the long-range effects on the children, but the suggestion has merit.

The prognosis for this type of abuser is very poor.

The Accidental or Unknowing Abuser

Most accidental abuse occurs only once. When it is reported the event is usually not denied by the abuser, and with many of this type, the treatment indicated is to assist the abuser in living with the consequences of his or her behavior. Most feel guilty, and all seem to be acutely aware of community responses, which are perceived as highly negative.

Those who are similar to the neglectful abuser in that they are mentally retarded must be handled in a manner that protects both the children and the parents. In those cases where poor parental judgment continues and unwitting abuse occurs, the goal must be protection of the child. Therapeutically, these abusers are difficult to work with because while they can be helped point by point and issue by issue to see the consequences to the child of an action, transfer of training seems lacking. In more prosaic terms we might say that it is difficult to teach good judgment, particularly if the abuser is at all retarded.

With the accidental abuser the prognosis is excellent. With the unwitting and unknowing abuser, the prognosis ranges from guarded to very poor.

Victim-Precipitated Abuse

In treating this type of abuse, the primary therapeutic effort must be focused on the child rather than the adult abuser. Children in this category have learned to precipitate violence in adults because particular behavior has been rewarded over a period of time. To modify and then alter this pattern of child-adult interaction it is necessary to reward the behavior that meets the child's needs but does not call forth violence in the adult caretakers. In simple terms, parents should be instructed to reward any behavior that appears desirable and to discourage the learned behavior patterns that precipitate violence by ignoring them. This sounds simple, but it is not. In fact, highly complex professional consultation and assistance are usually needed to develop a suitable reinforcement schedule. In addition, parental feelings can give rise to nonverbal cues that reinforce the undesired behavior at the same time as the desired behaviors are being praised verbally. These "mixed signals" often cause the child great difficulty and can only be detected through observing parental interaction with the child.

In the pathological model, these children are viewed as reminders to the abuser of a hated parent, stepparent, former spouse, brother, teacher, minister (or what have you). As a consequence of this view, these children are often placed in foster care or, worse, permanently placed with another family. Unfortunately, the child still carries its vulnerability with it to the new setting, and a replication of difficulties usually occurs. This view also implies that the primary problem is with the parent rather than the child and that placement in a foster setting with "warm, loving adults" will solve the situation. It does not.

The treatment of choice is to have the child remain in its own home and to offer the family "massive services": daily contact, perhaps more than once a day initially; and a great deal of observation of the child, the parents, and the parents and the child together. In the short run this is expensive and time-consuming but in the long run it is the most economical treatment. The combination of long-term foster care and professional time that effects little or no change in the child's vulnerability costs much more than intensive effort directed to the child and the parents for a relatively short time.

The prognosis is generally good for this type.

The Subcultural Abuser

This type of abuse is difficult to work with and difficult to treat. Since it is practiced by people who subscribe to violence as a desired trait, the therapist is "going against the grain" of a whole series of values and behavior that permeate the life style of the abuser. These values and this life style are reinforced not only in the relationship to the abuser's children but also by friends, coworkers, neighbors, and, in some respect, the entire society in which the abuser lives. Therapeutically, about the only thing that can be done is to work with the abuser to exempt the child from violence. Most subcultural abusers place a high value on children, and this is a trait that can be exploited therapeutically. When this value is used for leverage, some parents can be redirected to the point where their child-rearing practices fall within legal and societal norms.

In those cases where adults abuse children on religious grounds, the task is extremely difficult and, at times, hopeless. The abuse may range from horrible beatings to allowing children to die from lack of medical treatment to "prove faith in God." Subcultural abuse on religious grounds is so difficult to treat because the therapist is, in effect, "going against God," and the reader can understand who wins the contest.

In one instance, a little girl lay critically ill from heart disease. She was examined by a physician upon order of the court, and the findings were clear: Without immediate attention she would die. The court gave the parents *five days* to make a decision and, of course, the child died. The prosecuting attorney took the evidence before a grand jury and pointed out that a veterinarian had treated the parents' animals but medical care had been denied the child. Nothing happened to the parents, but the prosecutor was defeated in the next election, partly because he had taken the case before a grand jury!

Probably the only resolution for this type of abuse will be through legal processes. While Americans cherish religious freedom, we may have to make the distinction that all Americans must be guaranteed life, and this includes children. If parents wish to exercise their religious freedom and not use physicians themselves, we should not object. But when these beliefs deny other Americans (in this case their children), the right to life, society should immediately intervene on the children's behalf. After the children reach their legal majority, it would then become their right to decide whether they wish to test their faith by refusing medical treatment.

Another partial solution may be found in the ministry. Ministers can take a more active role with their congregations and inform them that severe punishment of children is not the Christian way of child rearing and that all life, including that of children, is sacred. Also, the medical profession might push for national and state legislation that will protect children.

It is unfortunate that we did not receive an Eleventh Commandment, "Honor thy children."

The Mentally Ill Abuser

When child abuse is a symptom of mental illness, resolution of the abuse will not come without resolution of the illness. It is fruitless to treat this one symptom, just as it is useless to treat a high fever due to appendicitis and ignore the inflamed appendix. In dealing with this type of abuser, several points should be clearly understood:

1. The mentally ill abuser may be extremely lethal.

2. Protection of the child is of paramount importance, in both the short and long range. Foster care, simply for protection of the child, is probably indicated more in this type than in any other, and adoptive placement of the child is also frequently indicated.

3. When mentally ill abusers are taking medication, it does not necessarily follow that they will not abuse their children.

4. When an agency charged with child protection "refers out" the mentally ill abuser to a mental health clinic, the agency is not absolved of moral if not legal responsibility for the child's life.

5. When a case is referred to a mental health agency or other professional, for the protection of the child a written memorandum of communications or the understanding should be prepared. This document should give the specific dates and times when interviews will be held, clarify the responsibility of each agency, and specify who will work with the child. This document should also specify the methods of communication, the frequency of agency communication, the frequency of home visits, and the notification of missed or cancelled appointments.

6. Under no circumstances should the life or well-being of the child be risked for "therapeutic reasons" to aid the mentally ill abuser. If a mental health professional tells the agency the mentally ill abuser needs the child so that he or she does not become sicker, the agency should refuse permission unless the professional making the request will state in writing that the abusive behavior will not be repeated.

This point is mentioned because several instances have come to the author's attention in which a mental health professional working with an abusive adult has stated that the patient will become worse unless he or she can have the child. After abuse has already occurred, it seems unethical if not criminal to use the child as a clinical tool.

7. A close working team is indicated. The needs of the men-

tally ill abuser must be met; the child must be protected, at the same time, any ill effects it may have experienced from its relationship to the abuser must be assessed and/or treated; and the two treatment plans must be closely and carefully coordinated. Treatment of the mentally ill abuser and the child is complex and difficult.

8. This type should be treated by mental health professionals in mental health clinics or hospitals, or by practitioners in psychology or psychiatry.

The prognosis for the Mentally Ill Abuser can range from very poor to very good, depending on the length of the illness and other individual aspects.

Institutionally Prescribed Abuse

This type of abuse differs from every other type in that individuals are carrying out approved and established policies. In many instances, if the policies are changed so will the individuals, and the abuse will cease.

Part of the "treatment" consists of exposing these practices, and exposure comes primarily from public scrutiny of all institutions. We really need the active involvement of laypersons and professionals whose interest in inmates in local, county, state, and federal institutions goes beyond a mere statement of concern. The news media have also very effectively exposed abusive practices in public and private schools and institutions. Individually and collectively they should be urged to continue their investigations.

The long-range solution of this problem will probably have to come from the courts and massive personal injury suits brought on behalf of the victims. Many school boards, principals, and teachers feel relatively comfortable when they have written permission from the parents for corporal punishment in their schools. This is a false sense of security, for many lawyers will argue that parents cannot give permission to assault a child. In any event, if one hits a child one is not legally absolved from the consequences of the act, with or without parental permission. Another questionable area is the set of rules for which corporal punishment is inflicted. Many are senseless, most restrict the development of children, and many if not most benefit the teacher or the principal rather than the children in their care. A few, of course, are based on teacher values as to what is "proper behavior." For example, we still have athletic coaches who believe that short hair is somehow connected with all that is good, and long hair with all that is bad.

Public education has been under attack over its stewardship of American children (McClung, 1974), but there are some healthy and hopeful legal signs on the horizon. There are still instances where the courts are more concerned with parental rights than with those of the children directly involved, as in *Wisconsin* v. *Yoder,* 406 U.S. 205 (1972). But in one of the many "long hair" cases the court moved beyond the simple issue at hand and took a brief view of the rights of children. In *Arnold* v. *Carpenter,* 459 F.2d939 (7 Cir. 1972), the court ruled that since hair is a constitutionally protected right, majority approval by the students of a code regulating hair length was irrelevant. Also thrown out, so to speak, was the provision exempting students who had parental consent. This position recognizes that children have certain rights, independent of parental wishes.

In the matter of abuse in licensed institutions such as day care centers, clearer and stricter licensing is obviously needed and indicated. One possible alternative is to change the administrative structure and responsibility for licensing from state departments of public welfare and their counterparts to the state attorney general's office. This would decrease the continuing pattern of permitting abuse while "social working" the abusive administrators. In any event, the function of licensing should be separated from that of professional service and consultation in attaining licensing goals.

The prognosis for the abolition of institutionally prescribed abuse in public schools in the next decade is fair. The prognosis for abolishing abuse in licensed day care centers and other child-rearing institutions within the next decade ranges from fair to excellent, depending on the activities of professional organizations such as the American Medical Association, the American Bar Association, the American Psychological Association, and the National Association of Social Workers.

There is every reason to believe that with increased scrutiny of schools by courts, corporal punishment will become a thing of the past. Attacks on corporal punishment will probably be based on the First and Fourteenth Amendments.

The Self-Identified Abuser

Successful treatment is easier to accomplish in this type than in any other in the typology. Self-identified abusers recognize that they have a problem in child rearing, are disturbed by their own and their children's behavior, and are motivated to do something about it. They respond well in groups and progress very rapidly, almost eagerly, to nonabusive patterns. Future parents or young parents who would like to explore possible alternatives to physical violence in child rearing might also fit into such groups.

Many self-identified abusers would probably step forward and seek help if professional help were available and if a stigma were not attached to the seeking of help. The prognosis for this group is excellent.

Effective treatment of abusive adults varies with the type of abuser with whom the professional is working. Some respond well to individual and/or group treatment, others respond less favorably, and some not at all. The primary goal of treatment in each instance should be protection of the child, with nonabusive child-rearing patterns the hope for the future. It does not matter very much initially how a parent feels, but how he or she acts.

Treatment is an ongoing human process in which the professional and the patient must jointly explore the problems and the goals. One is not superior and the other inferior. Rather, the therapist must attempt to convey a feeling of acceptance and caring for the patient as a person, without necessarily accepting the patient's behavior or the implications of that behavior. A viable treatment of choice seems to be groups that concentrate on identifying stress in the abuser, identifying children's behavior that precipitates abuse, and developing alternative (nonabusive) coping mechanisms.

CHAPTER EIGHT

Sexual Abuse of Children

Virtually no literature exists on the sexual abuse of children.
This problem is shrouded by misinformation, myths, and ignorance
in the lay and professional communities alike. Sex is a forbidden
topic among many people, and we will see that this taboo has had
far-reaching and damaging implications in understanding and treating sexual abuse.

Sexual abuse is substantively different from physical abuse of
children in the aetiology, occurrence, reporting, and, particularly,
the treatment of the problem. Sexual abuse is considered on the national reporting form of the Children's Division of the American
Humane Association (1974) as a type of physical abuse. It is not,
and to view it as such only confuses our understanding of both
phenomena.

Physical abusers are rarely treated; and it is safe to say that
sexual abusers are almost never treated. Treatment of the adult
who sexually abuses children is much more difficult for the therapist,
and successful treatment is beyond the capability of most public
welfare agencies, or others to whom sexual abuse is reported. It
may be helpful to examine some of the myths surrounding sexual
abuse of children, and to answer these myths with factual comments,
based upon experience.

Myths and Facts of Sexual Abuse

Myth: There is a universal, cross-cultural taboo against incest.
Fact: Several cultures permit incest and have encouraged it under

111

certain conditions. If the definition of incest includes brother-sister unions along with father-daughter and mother-son unions, the incidence of incest increases. The royal houses of both Egypt and Hawaii permitted incest.

In the United States we have strong prohibitions against incest, based on our Judeo-Christian heritage. To enforce the prohibition against incest some penalty must be paid for violation of the taboo, and the penalties—again myths—have been thoroughly incorporated into our culture.

Myth: If a child is born of parent-child sexual relationships it will be mentally retarded or have physical anomalies.
Fact: It may or may not, depending on the genetic factors of the father and mother. The author has interviewed three children of father-daughter liaisons. None had any physical anomalies, and all were enrolled in a university.

This fact has implications in treatment. In many instances professionals have decided in advance that the child of the union should be aborted or institutionalized upon birth. This is unfair to the child and its parents. Such a decision should only be made by the parents after consultation with a geneticist.

Myth: In most sex abuse cases, the abuser is a stranger to the child.
Fact: The sexual abuser, in the vast majority of instances, is well known to the child. He is usually a relative—such as a father, a brother-in-law, or an uncle—or a family friend or neighbor.
Many believe that the typical sexual abuser of children is a lecherous old man with candy bars, hiding in the bushes outside the local elementary school, or that it is some sex-crazed man driving around the neighborhood trying to entice young girls and boys into a car so that he can take them out in the country and sexually abuse them. Unfortunately, both do occur, and when they occur they are extremely newsworthy. Because they occur, children should be warned not to get into a stranger's car and to report suspicious individuals who approach them. It matters not whether the individual is a sexual abuser of children or a drug pusher; children should be

protected from both. But the pedophile and the man who tries to pick up children represent only a minuscule minority of all sexual abusers.

Myth: Sexual abuse of children is equally distributed between adult women who exploit young boys and adult men who exploit young girls.
Fact: Almost all the cases that are referred involve adult men and underage girls. When boys are abused or exploited they are usually the victims of adult males.

Myth: The lower the family income and social status the higher is the likelihood of sexual abuse of children.
Fact: There are no data to support this conclusion. It is safe to assume, however, that the lower the income and social status the higher the likelihood of being reported to a public agency rather than to a private practitioner.

Myth: Multiple sex abuse (such as a father abusing two or more daughters) is extremely rare.
Fact: If there are two or more daughters in the home, without discovery or intervention, a sexually abusive father will be involved with each of them. It is extremely rare for a father to be sexually abusing only one daughter if there are several in the family.

Myth: Psychologically, the sexually abused child is permanently damaged.
Fact: This need not be true. Most of the psychological damage, if any, stems not from the abuse but from the interpretation of the abuse and the handling of the situation by parents, medical personnel, law enforcement and school officials, and social workers.

Myth: The stigma of sexual abuse is placed only on the abuser, never on the child.
Fact: The child is likely to suffer more as a result of the abuse than the adult. Frequently, the child is thought to have "brought on" the

sexual abuse by being seductive and is stigmatized by her peers. Often it is necessary to place the child in a different school.

Myth: In the majority of cases, sexually abused children wish to leave their homes permanently.
Fact: On the contrary, most wish to remain in the home. Instances have even been seen in which the father, the daughter, and the mother are happy with the arrangement. The daughter usually has but one desire—that legal authorities permanently leave the home.

Myth: In father-daughter sexual involvement, the mother is unaware of sexual abuse occurring between the father and daughter.
Fact: In the majority of cases, the mother has good grounds to suspect the abuse, and she often contributes to its occurrence in a psychodynamic sense by leaving one daughter alone with the father. Upon discovery, though, more often than not the mother will insist that the daughter be removed from the home.

Myth: Usually when an adult male sexually abuses a child, the primary cause may be found in the relationship between the two.
Fact: The child is usually incidental. The primary cause of the sexual abuse usually rests in the relationship between the adult male and the adult female.

Myth: In the overwhelming majority of cases, sexually abusive adults are rapidly and expeditiously prosecuted, convicted, and sentenced.
Fact: If the abuser is a stranger to the child, prosecution does usually occur. But the vast majority of abusers are not strangers, as we have noted. Prosecution is rare, and this is not because prosecutors are not interested. Often neither the prosecutor nor the police are informed. If prosecution is brought, it is hampered because children make poor witnesses and many times the family refuses to testify.

Myth: Sexual abuse of children is a clear violation of the laws protecting children.
Fact: There are very few laws covering sexual abuse of children,

and most of them are vague and unenforceable. Even most state incest laws are inadequate. The problem of prosecution becomes even more difficult when the abuse is a mutually agreed-upon event.

Myth: Any father who would sexually abuse or be involved with his daughter must be mentally ill.
Fact: Few are mentally ill. The vast majority hold jobs, function well in the community, and are fairly well respected by their peers. Some claim alcoholic intoxication and loss of memory of the event. Others claim seduction by the child. Most deny the event, and most feel it is none of society's business. But usually they are not mentally ill.

Myth: Sexual abuse is easy to treat, once it becomes known.
Fact: Sexual abuse is extremely difficult to treat because it involves three people moving at different speeds. Often none of the three are motivated for treatment. Some actually are extremely resistive to treatment.

These common myths are subscribed to by many laypersons and some members of the professional community, mostly because they tend to reinforce the biblical injunctions against incest and support current mores if abuse does occur.

Extent of Sexual Abuse of Children

What is the extent of sexual abuse of children in America? No one knows. Sexual abuse is usually considered a family problem, and when it is discovered, it quickly becomes a family secret and is not mentioned to an outsider. Even those instances that should be fairly simple to document (a stranger molesting a child) are kept hidden. Further, other than for outright fondling of genitalia, it becomes highly problematical as to whether abuse has occurred. If a stranger "talks dirty" to a child, is it sexual abuse? Probably yes, but this would be very difficult to prove in a court of law. If an uncle tells a 14- or 15-year-old girl, "You certainly are developing well," is that abuse? It may be inappropriate behavior, but it is unlikely that it is abuse.

One university professor asked the author to see his 11-year-old daughter because of her problem. When asked for details, the father complained, "She no longer likes to take baths with me." Who has the problem, the maturing daughter, aware of her sexuality, or the father? Then we might ask, if he insists that she continue to bathe with him, is he sexually abusing her? Another father installed a one-way mirror in the bathroom so he could observe his daughters taking showers. Was he sexually abusive?

Thus we see that problems in reporting and in definition compound our difficulties in determining the extent of the problem.

Most approaches made by adults to boys are of a homosexual nature, while those made to girls are usually heterosexual. Most children are able to cope with these approaches without lasting trauma. In an attempt to make a rough assessment of the problem, the author asked 412 university freshmen and sophomores to complete a brief questionnaire about their experiences in the period prior to puberty. They were asked what sexual "signals" were given to them by adults when they were children and whether these "signals" were verbal, physical, or a combination of the two. The last question of the questionnaire asked if the respondent would agree to be interviewed in confidence if additional information were needed. The results were somewhat surprising and interesting:

1. Twenty-one percent responded that they had received verbal signals or approaches of some sort from adults, and 17 percent reported some type of physical contact.

2. All sexual signals received by female respondents came from adult males, and male respondents reported overwhelmingly that sexual signals were received from adult males. Only one instance was found of an adult female who attempted to exploit both girls and boys.

3. Those who made sexual advances to the female respondents were well known and related to them by blood and/or marriage. Frequently reported were uncles and brothers-in-law. Some reported advances made by adult male neighbors.

4. Among male respondents, homosexual advances were made by adult males who were not related by blood or marriage but were fairly well known to them. Those making approaches ranged from camp counselors, adult males at church functions, corner grocers, teachers, and, in one instance, a volunteer working with the boy.

5. The vast majority of contacts did not seem to cause lasting effect or damage to the respondents. Most seemed to accept it simply as a distasteful, puzzling, or normal event in their development. But also, most of the contact consisted in asking the child to view or feel a penis or to be rubbed, caressed, or fondled in what was perceived to be a sexually stimulating or rewarding way for the adult. Among females, instances of adult males' touching the child's genitalia were reported in 50 percent of the cases in which physical contact occurred.

As with most questionnaires distributed in university classes, the contents became known through dormitory conversations. The author was quite surprised by the nearly twenty students who contacted him to volunteer information about their own childhoods and sexual experiences with adults that had left them angry and disturbed. In each instance, the student had had some type of physical experience in which there was no question of the meaning of the adult's intentions or behavior.

This very loosely organized attempt to measure the extent of sexual abuse indicates that the problem does exist and that organized, systematic research on many populations is necessary to ascertain the size of the problem. No conclusions can be drawn from this preliminary survey as the questions were vague and the population was limited to social science university underclassmen on three campuses of two midwestern universities. What is needed is a valid and reliable instrument to obtain data on sexual abuse from a representative sample of the United States. This instrument should include the pubescent years and not be restricted to the prepubescent years. Until such research is under way, we must be aware that sexual abuse of children is commoner than most people suspect and that only a very few cases are reported.

Most sexual abuse is not reported because it involves family or friends of the family. The usual chain of events seems to be that the child who is approached or abused sexually tells an older sibling, who relays the information to the mother, who tells the father. The mother is disturbed, but the father is enraged and frequently threatens to kill or otherwise harm the abuser. Because a family member or a close friend is involved, "cooler heads prevail" lest the family "be disgraced," and the event is never mentioned again. The offender is kept away from the children or the abuser is closely watched at occasions such as family reunions. The event is not discussed with the child after the details are elicited. The child frequently feels guilty or responsible for a disruption in the family, but never has the opportunity to discuss his or her feelings.

Sexual Abuse Reported to Public Agencies

Sexual abuse of children as reported to public agencies differs substantively from overall abuse in the United States. In working with or consulting on more than 2,000 abuse cases, the author has found the following:

1. Physical abuse referrals overwhelmingly outnumber sexual abuse referrals.

2. Most sexual abuse referrals involve underage girls.

3. The most frequently reported abusers are natural fathers, stepfathers, and mothers' boyfriends.

4. In only three out of more than 200 sexual abuse cases was an adult female reported for sexually abusing a child. In all three instances, the victims were boys.

5. It is extremely rare for the abuser to be prosecuted. Prosecution is resisted by the victim, the mother, and any others involved. Most professionals know of cases in which a daughter has been impregnated and has borne her father's child, yet charges have not been filed.

A vaginal examination is frequently made to determine whether the girl has had sexual relationships, and instances can be cited where the examination has been scheduled one or two weeks after the suspected abuse or even later. As the majority of physicians will attest, this is ridiculous. Why agencies who are charged with protecting children allow this sort of thing to happen is difficult to understand.

Another abuse of the child occurs in polygraph examinations. If the father obtains an attorney, or if the police become involved, the child often becomes the "accused" and the suspected abuser the "victim." The girl must take a lie detector test to see if she "is telling the truth." Leaving the question of the worth of the lie detector aside, we must take an objective view of the situation. The girl who was victimized now must bear the burden of proof. If she "fails" the test, the suspected abuser is exonerated. If she "passes" the test it proves nothing. It seems more advisable to give the adult the polygraph test, for, after all, he is the accused, but this does not occur very often. The whole procedure says something about the rights and status of children vis-à-vis those of adults.

A rather common myth mentioned earlier claims that if a girl is sexually abused as a youngster, disaster will follow. Some think she will become sterile, homosexual, nymphomaniac, criminal, mentally ill, or meet some other dire fate as a result of the experience. This is simply not true. The abuse itself rarely does long-lasting damage; it is how the abuse is handled that seems to make the difference.

If parents become upset and speak, as in one instance, of "the horrible thing done to you," in all probability the child will feel it is horrible. Similarly, in a hospital one child overheard a detective saying that the little girl's father "should be shot for what he did to Lisa." This was traumatic. But if the people in contact with the child handle the matter well and in a sensitive manner, the harm can be greatly minimized.

The author has worked with women who have been sexually abused as children and upon maturity have dismissed the childhood event by saying, "Dad was 'sick' [mentally ill] when he did that, but he is all right now."

Similarly, in the case of a 7-year-old boy whose penis was nearly chewed off by a man of the cloth at a church camp, the parents handled it well. The boy was treated medically and experienced some pain, but his parents were warm, supporting, and loving toward the child. Without minimizing the event, they responded only to the child's questions and did not offer him their own interpretation. Relatives and friends who knew of the event were asked not to mention it to the child or to quiz him. The detective assigned to the case spent several days with the boy in the hospital, developing a very warm relationship before he began gently and sensitively to question him. The parents elected not to prosecute the offender, feeling (and rightly so) that a court appearance and cross-examination would probably be too upsetting to the child. Seven years later the child displays no signs of maladjustment and has not mentioned the event since therapy was terminated, some six years ago.

Unfounded or Baseless Accusations of Sexual Abuse by Children

Instances of false accusations of sexual abuse have resulted in a cautious approach to any accusation by a child and have permitted many agencies and professionals to avoid facing up to real and known instances of abuse by adults.

Upon discovery and report, sexual abuse becomes an adversary proceeding. The adult is more verbal, has better-developed defenses, and is assumed innocent until proven guilty. The child, on the other hand, is viewed with a great deal of suspicion, and external proofs, such as semen or physical damage to the child, must usually be present. Even with physical damage, the child's reliability is often doubted. For example, a girl of 4 who was hospitalized with massive internal damage was asked by an emergency room nurse, "Were you 'playing' with yourself?"

Accusations by teen-age girls are often lacking in substance or foundation. But in taking a quasi-legal adversary approach to the accusation, we miss the whole point of abuse and treatment. The fact that sexual abuse did not occur, in no way diminishes the need for treatment, and those agencies that close out a reported sexual abuse case by saying the complaint was unfounded have been derelict in meeting their obligations.

All children have problems with their parents. Boys learn at an early age how to "handle" mothers, and girls learn how to "handle" fathers. Some girls sit on Daddy's lap when they want something and tell him how handsome he is—a sure winner in most instances. When frustrated and angry, some girls cry and try to make their fathers feel guilty. Others run to their rooms and refuse to eat because they are not allowed to go to a rock concert, or they assume the "martyr role." Boys, too, have their arsenal of techniques to control their mothers.

Very, very few children accuse a parent of being sexually involved with them. When that does occur, whether the accusation is founded or unfounded, by its very rarity we may suspect a severe disruption in the relationship between a daughter and her father or a son and his mother. It really does not matter whether the abuse occurred or not; treatment is still indicated.

The Father-Daughter Involvement

We can best understand why sexual abuse occurs by looking at the most typical situation: a father who is involved with his daughter. The beginning student can best understand this involvement as the father's ultimate act of hostility or hatred toward the mother. In everyday common terms, let us assume that the reader is married or has taken up a long-term commitment to another, which has resulted in a child. If your husband/wife were to become sexually involved with another person, would you prefer that that person be another adult or your child? The answer, universally, is another adult. We must then ask why one selects one's child. An adult has or can create all kinds of opportunities for sexual involvement with another adult, for adult partners are available in every community. The basic reason for being involved with one's child is anger toward one's spouse.

Sexual abuse then, involves all three members of the triad: the adult male, the adult female, and the child. This fact has many implications in the treatment of sexual abuse, which is discussed in the next chapter.

The Father in the Sexual Abuse Triad. To repeat, most sexually abusive fathers and stepfathers are fairly well respected by their peers *before* it becomes known in the community that they were sexually involved with their daughters. When the news is out, a rapid reevaluation occurs, and former friends and associates will suddenly cite "peculiarities" of life style or personality that tend to place the abuser apart from the observer. Common reactions are "Now that I think about it, he was quiet and never mentioned his home"; "I thought he was drinking too much"; "I believe he mentioned once there was a history of insanity in his family"; "He had a terrible childhood"; or "It must have been the war that affected him." This is a common phenomenon indulged in by friends, family, and neighbors. The remarks are usually picked up by professionals, who are also seeking something that will set the father apart or trying to find some causal agent in the background that may "explain" the abusive event. When a reason is found (and one always is) everyone can view the father as "sick" and in need of treatment. All the attention is then focused on the father.

If the father protests his innocence, the same process occurs with respect to the daughter. Her school performance, interaction with her peers, appearance, attractiveness, medical and family history —all come under scrutiny in order to assess her complicity in the event as well as her truthfulness.

Many sexually abusive fathers are described as "tyrants" in the home after the abuse is reported, sometimes "violent and unpredictable." This, of course, further reinforces the father's complete responsibility for the event, while the daughter and the wife are considered helpless prisoners of a despotic, sexually abusive father. Professionals who have worked with sexual abuse frequently encounter a father who has been described in these terms. When he enters the office for an interview, the professional is astonished to find this "violent and unpredictable" man to be 5'7", 150 lbs., and neatly dressed. He is of a calm disposition and appears to be a rather anxious, harassed, and overburdened man, puzzled by recent events. This is not to say that there are not tyrannical and despotic fathers, for there are fathers of this type; but more often than not, the sexually abusive father is given this label unjustly to explain away any and all involvement of other members of the triad.

A somewhat rare but not unknown type is the sexually abusive father who appears to be pansexual. A pansexual is one who imbues all events in his or her life with erotic sexual feeling. One professional aptly described a pansexual father by saying, "It doesn't matter whether it is a cat, the telephone pole, the mailman, or his children. He gets 'turned on' by everything and anything." These men are rare but they do exist, and they are different from the usual sexually abusive father.

In terms of sexuality most abusive fathers appear to be rather conservative. They are not "oversexed," and, frequently, the therapist will learn that they have had but limited sexual experiences in childhood and marriage. Few have had homosexual experiences, and few believe in any type of sex that involves what they perceive as "perversions," such as cunnilingus or other variations of sexual practices.

The Wife/Mother in the Sexual Abuse Triad. In most instances, the wife/mother is viewed as "the innocent victim" of the sexual abuse situation. Sometimes, particularly if a stepfather is involved, she will report the abuse and seek prosecution. But if the natural father is involved, she usually becomes very protective of the suspected abuser, and if the sexual abuse is not denied, projects all the blame on the daughter. Given the choice of who is to remain in the home, the daughter or the husband, the wife will invariably select the husband.

In most instances, she plays the role expected of the aggrieved, unsuspecting victim of an event of which she had no prior knowledge. She will continue to play this role, even when faced with the evidence that the daughter attempted to or actually did bring the situation to the attention of the mother many times in the past. In playing out this role, the mother will often publicize the suspected or real sexual abuse to neighbors, relatives, ministers, and other members of her peer group. This is an attempt to reinforce the role assumed, and it often severely complicates the problem for each member of the triad.

Because she intuitively reacts to the dynamics of the event (the ultimate act of repudiation of her as a wife and sexual partner) one can expect her to state, "I don't know why he did that. I was always available" (for sexual involvement). The wife/mother usually comes from what she will describe as "just an average, but close family" background. She will describe her dating pattern as fairly normal. Occasionally she will allow that at some time in her marriage she was unfaithful to her husband, but that was "a long time ago and has been forgotten."

Usually, the marriage has been anything but harmonious, and the abuse event becomes the justification for separation or divorce for a couple who had long considered their marriage "dead." They have remained together "for the sake of the children" or because of the fear of the consequences of a breakup. In many instances, there are long-standing disagreements over personal values, finances, child rearing, food, clothing, and every other aspect of life. More often than not, the couple have not had sexual relationships for a year or more. This is not to paint the picture of a home with arguments, violence, and a sexually frustrated male, all of which culminate in an act of sexual abuse, for this is rarely seen. Rather, arguments are few and far between. Differences in opinions and values are not resolved; they are not even discussed. Long ago the couple reached some sort of accommodation, but it had no effect on the increase in the unvoiced hostility between them.

A few wife/mothers are "psychological invalids," who have played a passive-dependent role for years as a result of imagined physical problems without medical foundation. Still others have, for psychological or material reasons, become very unattractive as women, homemakers, wives, and human beings. There are also a few cases in which, because of the needs of both husband and wife, the woman becomes in every respect the husband's mother. A cultural taboo then makes the wife/mother as unapproachable sexually as the husband/father's own mother. The father then dynamically becomes an adolescent, and the sexually abused child is symbolically either his sister or his girlfriend. This phenomenon can be observed not only in discussing the relationship but also in the actual interaction. The author has seen instances of the husband's addressing the wife as "Mom" or "Mommy" and literally asking her for permission to go to the bathroom. Only upon discovery do the members of the triad resume their true roles, and then only superficially.

While the wife/mother nearly always denies knowledge of the involvement of the father and the daughter, in therapy she will either admit to knowing of the sexual abuse or relate that she "felt uncomfortable" or "suspicious" that the abuse was occurring. It is not uncommon either for the wife/mother to tacitly assist the father in his abusive endeavors.

The Child/Daughter in the Sexual Abuse Triad. There are instances, of course, in which the daughter competes with the mother for the sexual attentions of the adult male. This can frequently be observed in the relationship between an adolescent daughter and a stepfather who is older than the daughter but younger than the wife/mother. There are also young girls who seduce older men, as well as the reverse. This represents one type of situation in sexual abuse, and while it is not uncommon, it differs from the traditional incestuous relationship of the natural father–natural mother–natural daughter triad.

In most of the classic instances of sexual abuse, at a fairly early age the daughter begins play with sexual overtones with her father. The play progresses over a period of years, and this is an important point. The abuse does not develop overnight, and instances of a father's attacking a daughter sexually with no prior involvement are extremely rare. Often the father and the daughter have been engaging in various forms of sexual behavior over the years. They may begin by sleeping together; then the daughter is asked to fondle the father's penis or to masturbate him; as the daughter matures he may fondle her genitalia; and finally there is intercourse.

The daughter usually knows the father's behavior is "wrong." Her father's warning not to tell anyone implies wrongdoing, and even when she has not been warned, she does not tell her friends or playmates. Many times the daughter will either tell or attempt to tell the mother by hinting at what is transpiring, but these signals are ignored for the most part.

Sexual abuse is sometimes reported by daughters. It occurs when they are young if there is physical damage that requires medical treatment, but it happens most frequently at puberty. A teenage daughter can become quite resentful of the involvement with her father and will actively seek to break the bond. With or without this resentment, she may continue the relationship with the father to forestall his sexual involvement with a younger sister. When that happens (and it always does), the older daughter will then report the father to the authorities.

As mentioned earlier, when a girl reports her father for abuse the complaint is viewed with suspicion and mistrust, simply because some girls make unfounded accusations. But when a victim of abuse has straightforwardly reported her father and explained that she is doing so to protect a younger sister, she is frequently viewed with distaste as well as suspicion. The usual interpretation—that she is jealous of the younger sister and that she cannot stand to lose the sexual attention of the father—only clouds the issue and prevents understanding the situation. Professionals should recognize that there are girls who intensely dislike their fathers yet continue their involvement in a rather misguided but understandable way to "protect" a younger sister.

Many girls who have been sexually involved with their fathers seem to have a built-in defense of anger or some other mechanism that protects them from lasting harm from the experience. Some difficulties may arise when they date, and a time for particular concern is when they enter into a long-term commitment with a man. If the family is still in close contact with the therapist, working with the young woman and her mate is indicated before marriage.

Many girls are, in the truest sense of the word, their fathers' lovers. Many have the same type of relationship that adults have, and some resent community intervention. These cases are difficult to work with, particularly when professionals carry over a cultural bias that incest is wrong and that by definition the girls should resent it.

Other Forms of Sexual Abuse

Male Child–Adult Female. This type of sexual abuse is rare and we have only suggestions as to why it does not occur. One possible explanation is the purely physical aspect of intercourse. A daughter may be physically receptive to the adult male (or at least capable of sexual relationships), while the male must have an erection and maintain it. Perhaps because of cultural bias and values, the male child would be guilt-ridden and unable to produce an erection. Another explanation may be that the child at one time was physically part of the mother's body, not just the result of the father's contribution of sperm, and that the meaning of the child is different to the mother than to the father. Still another explanation may be found in our cultural biases about sexuality and the role of females in American society. In any event, there is no research on the topic, and the rarity of this type of abuse remains unexplained.

Adult women do seduce adolescent boys who are "willing victims," just as adult men seduce women who are "willing victims." If we were to label this behavior as sexual abuse, we would be on very shaky ground. For example, many teen-age boys visit prostitutes. Does this mean the prostitute should be charged with the sexual abuse of children? Or is the 18- or 21-year-old female who has sexual relations with a boy of 15 to be considered as sexually abusing him? Many difficult problems in definition arise in this particular area. The definition of sexual abuser should probably be restricted to adult women who are mothers or stepmothers, and the age of the victim, along with his maturity, should be considered in determining whether sexual abuse has occurred.

The following are three instances of reported sexual abuse of this type:

Ms. R. was a single parent with a 3-year-old boy. She would rub his penis against her genitals and had done this since the child was a few months old. She was reported to the police for allegedly teaching the boy to perform cunnilingus on her. She did not deny the charge.

Mrs. M. and her 15-year-old son had slept together since the father left home seven years earlier. Under the guise of "teaching [the boy] sex education," Mrs. M. masturbated her son and asked that he in turn do the same for her. She had sex relations with him a number of times, and was reported by an uncle in whom the boy had confided.

Mrs. J. was married to an Air Force pilot who was assigned overseas for a three-year tour. She and her 14-year-old stepson "got in a lovers' quarrel in a restaurant" and were reported. Investigation revealed that the 32-year-old stepmother had been having relations with the boy for nearly a year.

In the truest sense of the word, because of age, circumstances, and relationships, these cases can be considered sexual abuse. Again, while statistically rare, sexual abuse of boys by adult caretakers can occur.

Brother-Sister. Problems in this area are not reported as often as most laypersons assume. It is rare for an older brother to force a younger sister into sexual relations. The author has never encountered a case of an older sister seducing a younger brother, nor have any of his colleagues documented such a case. That is not to say it does not occur, only that it is rare.

Among many brothers and sisters, there is normal curiosity at an early age about the physical makeup of the opposite sex, and this can continue for some time. But because of the very nature of the totality of the natural brother-sister relationship, sexual involvement is quite rare.

The most common types of reported sexual abuse in brother-sister relationships occur between stepbrothers and stepsisters, particularly if they became related at a fairly advanced age. It is difficult and probably unwise to label many of these cases as sexual abuse, for the partners are related only through their respective parents' marriage. In one instance, "sexual abuse" by a 16-year-old brother of a 15-year-old stepsister was reported. Upon investigation, it was learned that the girl's father and boy's mother had married six months earlier. In this instance, we really are dealing with two normal teen-age children who are housed together. To tell them they should behave "as brother and sister" at that advanced age and to leave them unsupervised for long periods of time is simply inviting sexual behavior. It is erroneous to call this "sexual abuse."

Child Prostitution. Some instances are known where parents, stepparents, or older siblings prostitute a young girl. Justification for the practice stems from poverty or the advanced development and maturation of the child. These explanations must be viewed as rationalizations for differing value systems, rather than as suitable explanation for the behavior, for the overwhelming majority of poor people in America would never think of prostituting their daughters, no matter how impoverished they are.

An evolutionary process may occur in some situations where the family members are fairly promiscuous or sexually active beginning at an early age. After being involved with neighbors or cousins, the fairly experienced girl may move on to "turning tricks" for money, and be assisted in locating "marks" or "scores" by a brother or another male.

Adult Male–Male Child. All of us know of the horror connected with a mentally ill person, such as the one in Florida in 1973 who committed sexual acts with young boys and girls which resulted in the murder of one, or the bizarre and frightening Texas murders of an untold number of young boys. Whether the act is committed by a demented sadist is incidental; the fact is that events such as these cause great revulsion.

It must be added that those most revolted by such horrors are homosexuals themselves, who (rightly) feel that public acceptance of all homosexuals suffers from the acts of a few demented people. The converse, of course, is not true; all heterosexuals are not tarred by the same brush when one of them commits heinous acts.

Most boys come into contact with older homosexual men during the course of their childhood and during high school years. Many not only know them but also attempt to exploit older men for money, and are frequently successful in doing so. Just as many older males are attracted to young females, so are some adult homosexuals at-

tracted to young boys. But the majority of homosexuals, like heterosexuals, do not seek young partners.

An older male who exploits a young male for sexual purposes
should be prosecuted, just as an older male who exploits a young
female would be prosecuted for rape, for young males should also
be afforded the protection of rape laws.

In many instances of adult male–male child sexual abuse, a
close examination of the child's role reveals parental neglect and a
lack of concern over the comings and goings of teen-age boys.

Adults Who Expose Themselves and Pedophiles. There are
some relatively harmless adult males who cannot relate to adult males
or females, have doubts about their own sexuality, and who expose
themselves to others, sometimes to children. The usual community
reaction is severe censure if a child is involved, and more frequently
than not the offender is committed to a mental hospital voluntarily
or by his family.

Children are not traumatized by a "flasher" and frequently accept the behavior with better grace than do their parents. Any
trauma, as in most sexual abuse, comes from adult interpretation
and handling of the event. When parents get upset and a police drag-
net is instituted, the commotion often causes much more concern to
the child than the event itself.

Many parents are so fearful of an adult's exposing himself or
making a sexual advance toward a child, that they make their children fearful and suspicious of all adults they do not know extremely
well. Sadly, most of them do not know why they are not to get into
a stranger's car or accept gifts.

A change has occurred in America over the last two decades.
Many grandfathers are now fearful, particularly in public, that their
normal affections for their grandchildren will be misinterpreted by
others. Further, many male senior citizens are viewed with suspicion
when interacting with children because of the mistaken idea that a
"dirty old man" lurks in every bush, attempting to entice children.

Without minimizing the fact that pedophiles do indeed exist, it
would seem that the problem has become greatly distorted. Ten or
fifteen years ago, near one southern university, a much-loved and

respected elderly gentleman used to pass out his own home-grown flowers to children, high school girls, and girl students at the university. Today he would probably be arrested or at least reported several times a day.

Emotional

"Emotional Abuse" Connected with Sexuality. Recently some professionals have asked whether exposure to pornographic films constitutes "sexual abuse" of children or "emotional abuse" of children in the area of sexuality. Much has been said on both sides of this question, and some professionals are even including literature with obscene words in this category.

These are areas in which specialists in child abuse should not get involved. Calling the viewing of a pornographic movie or the reading of a book containing profanity or obscenities "sexual abuse of children" is a perversion and corruption not only of the terms, but also of professional roles.

It is true that the viewing of violence or of sexual acts in a film or the reading of material including both may, for certain children, be damaging and precipitate unwanted behavior, attitudes, and values. But on the other hand, children are emotionally abused in sexual areas every day because of repressive, guilt-ridden, punitive ideas that are transmitted to them under the guise of sex education. Let us look at some not uncommon examples of this teaching:

1. Masturbation is harmful and may result in brain damage or insanity. In instances known to the author, children were told, "You will grow webs between your fingers like a duck," and "Your 'thing' will rot off."

2. Females are unclean during their menstrual periods (from the Bible), and sexual relations should not occur during menstruation, which is sometimes referred to as "the curse."

3. Sexual relations before marriage are sinful, and sexual feelings should be denied until marriage.

4. The only purpose of sexual relations is procreation, and sex should not be a pleasurable experience in any event.

5. Intercourse other than in the "missionary position" (i.e., with the male on top and the female on her back) is "wrong."

The fact of the matter is that more "emotional abuse" in the area of sexuality occurs through lack of information and misinformation than by exposure to salacious material. Often, those who cry the loudest that sex education should occur in the home and not in the school are the very ones who provide misinformation or no information at all. The majority of American children are not taught anything about their own bodies, insofar as sex is concerned. Indeed, some reach adulthood not knowing that babies are the result of sexual relations!

CHAPTER NINE

Treatment of Sexual Abuse

Currently, only a small number of sexual abusers of children are treated, and for the most part the treatment is ineffective. There are several reasons for this deficiency:

1. Sexual abuse is hard to prove and easy to deny. It is a problem that is under-reported, hidden from public view, and contained in secrecy in many families. Discovery is usually accidental rather than purposive and depends on one member of the triad bringing it to the attention of the community.

2. Children in America are largely without legal rights, and a report from a child is viewed with suspicion and mistrust by most authorities. This suspicion is not without foundation in some cases, but because of the inferior role of children, legal and social authorities often respond in a manner that results in the child's retracting the accusation. The doubts of the adults and the inferiority of the child are seen in the insistence on vaginal, psychological, psychiatric, and lie detector examinations of the victim, or alleged victim, of sexual abuse.

3. When sexual abuse occurs within a family, attention is focused on the adult male who is abusing, to the exclusion of the adult female and the child. The typical response is not therapeutic but legal, and all efforts are directed toward building a case for prosecution of the offender. The abuser usually responds by retaining counsel, and he is often advised not to discuss the events or situation with anyone; thus meaningful treatment is precluded.

4. In those instances in which treatment is sought, the therapists often focus on the behavior (usually called the "pathology") of the male abuser to the exclusion of that of the other members of the triad.

5. Sexual abuse cannot be treated unless the abuse complaint is discussed or without talking about sex. While this point should be obvious to the most casual observer, in most instances neither the complaint nor the sexual attitudes, behavior, and familial relationships are dealt with in any depth. There is a normal reluctance to discussing the complaint and dealing with a taboo topic, and therefore therapists and patients alike tend to focus on extraneous matters such as income and early childhood. Not infrequently, those charged with treating sexual abuse are more comfortable than their patients when discussing sexual matters.

6. Many agencies seem to believe in treatment by osmosis; that is, by discussing the sexual abuse with the adult female or the child, somehow, indirectly, they think they are treating the sexually abusive male. In the same vein, some male therapists have directed their efforts toward the male abuser, thinking that that will produce change in the adult female or the child.

7. Treatment efforts are one-to-one, uncoordinated, and based on an analytical model that suggests that the sexual abuse occurred because of traumatic events in early childhood, rather than being due to an impoverishment of relationship between the adults involved.

8. The motivation for therapy is often the avoidance of the legal consequences of sexual abuse. When the case is dismissed, nol-prossed, or otherwise removed from the criminal justice system, the sexual abuser often views this as a vindication of his position and terminates the therapy.

9. Many agencies charged with treating as well as investigating sexual abuse complaints attempt treatment and the discussion of sexual matters in the patient's home. Homes have different meanings to different people. In many instances, sex has never been discussed (and virtually nothing else has either) in homes where sexual abuse has occurred. Further, when interviews are held in homes,

the therapeutic atmosphere changes. In contrast to office interviews, the client rather than the therapist is literally on "home ground" and assumes control of the relationship.

10. Pressures are exerted on the sexual abuser for a nontherapeutic resolution of the problem. These pressures are generated by families, neighbors, friends, and sometimes officials of the criminal justice system. Among the nontherapeutic resolutions that are frequently seen and reinforced are: religious conversion or rededication, forsaking alcohol, moving to a new or old locality, "starting life and the marriage anew," changing jobs, changing spouses, and—one that is suggested by some professionals charged with treating sexual abuse—changing sleeping arrangements.

How then might we or should we treat the sexual abuser of children? If the abuse did in fact occur, our immediate goal should be to insure that it does not recur. The long-range goal is the same even if the abuse did not occur, that is, a change to healthier familial relationships, to the point where sex is not used as a controlling mechanism in parent-child interaction) This may mean a restructuring not only of the relationships between the parents and the child involved but, as is needed in the vast majority of cases, of all the family relationships and interrelationships. The multiple triads, encompassing the other children in the household, must be included in this restructuring.

The immediate goal—a cessation of further sexual involvement between adult and child—is fairly easy to accomplish. The long-range goal is much more complex and difficult to achieve.

Initial Approach in Sexual Abuse

As in physical abuse, the professional to whom the suspected sexual abuse case is referred must contact the child and the family and inform the suspected abuser of the allegation. All parties involved should be given the name of the person interviewing them and the agency he or she represents, and an appointment should be made for a followup interview the next day, even if it means rearranging a schedule.

Denial of the sexual abuse is to be expected, and the person handling the case would be ill advised to "play detective." To do so might meet the ego needs of the professional, but it is inimical to long-range treatment. Rather, the person handling the complaint should approach the alleged abuser and the members of the triad as humans and individuals. Depending on the circumstances surrounding the initial report and referral, it is often advisable to approach the victim first. A rapid assessment can be made as to whether the child should remain in the home or whether the suspected abuser or the child should be removed temporarily.

The approach to all concerned must be professional, but warm. Participants are not "suspects" or "subjects"; they are people. If the approach is policelike or investigative in tone, there is every reason to believe that the participants will behave like impersonal "suspects" or "subjects." If the complaint is received from a hospital emergency room the professional must be acutely aware of his or her role and should not assist or support the police in gathering data, interrogation, or any other activities they engage in with an eye toward prosecution. That is not the role of therapist.

Whether the alleged abuser admits or denies the sexual involvement is not important in the early contact. One of the simplest ways to convince parents of the need for treatment is to point out that with the wide array of choices available, most girls do not accuse a parent of sexual abuse and that the accusation perhaps shows a need to strengthen and sort out family relationships. Most parents will not and cannot argue with this point.

It is imperative that a date for an office interview be established immediately. If the participants cannot keep the appointment because of job or other commitment, the professional must stress by words and action that the problem is the most important and far-reaching crisis in the family. It may well determine the future of each participant, the relationships among them, and the community's reaction to the event.

Early Treatment of Sexual Abuse

In many instances, the professional must protect the child and both adults from the community and from themselves. This does not mean that the professional should encourage them not to mention the matter to others, but he or she should point out the long-range consequences of the real or alleged event. A complaint of sexual abuse will remain in the family history for the lifetime of those involved. It is not a matter to be taken lightly, and it is one that not only requires assistance directly to the family but also other efforts on its behalf.

Family relationships are strained. Often, the suspected abuser believes that the wife or daughter "betrayed" him. At this time a real service can be provided to each individual and to the family as a group by permitting open and honest ventilation and articulation of feelings. Many times the victim bears the brunt of the feelings. Sometimes one of the adult's extended family will try to exert pressure on the child. This frequently happens when the victim is hospitalized, and so it is often wise not to allow visitors outside the immediate family. If aunts, grandparents, and cousins are permitted to visit, someone else should be present at all times to prevent any interrogation of the child and to control the content and process of the visit. Medical social workers employed by the hospital are particularly adept in this area and should be given full knowledge of the situation.

When all members of the triad and perhaps other children remain in the home, one way of trying to prevent future sexual abuse is outright recognition of the complaint with all members of the triad. The professional can say to the father, "If you feel the situation may recur, or that any of your actions may be misinterpreted, call me as soon as possible"; to the mother, "If you suspect this will recur, call me immediately"; and to the child, "If you think it is going to recur, tell your mother and call me immediately." It is best to give these instructions to each member of the triad in the presence of the others. The professional must then be available at all times and accessible by phone at the office, at home, or through an answering service. This approach has been criticized for making everyone in the home wary of everyone else and for placing too much stress on the role of the professional as a problem solver, rather than letting the family resolve its own problems. The answer to this criticism is that this measure is only an initial step to forestall future sexual involvement, that in most instances the members of the triad are already suspicious of one another, and that since the family obviously has not been able to solve its problems satisfactorily, for a short time dependence on a professional is not therapeutically wrong. Finally, this approach has the advantages of bringing the sexual abuse complaint, whether founded or not, into the open.

At the outset, the professional should explain the agency's role, answer any questions, and clarify in advance the agency's connection, if any, with legal authorities. Sometimes it is prudent not to delve too deeply into whether the abuse occurred until the legal authorities have made their disposition. In many jurisdictions, information given to agency personnel by a sexual abuser and other members of the triad is not privileged. Each member of the triad should be informed of this fact, for it is unfair for them to confide in a professional only to find out later that that person is in court, under subpoena to testify as to what was said. There have been instances where the defense attorney and the prosecutor felt that treatment of the family was most important, and a "gentleman's agreement" has been made so that the professional working with the family would not be called as a witness.

In sexual abuse as much as in physical abuse, attorneys are human and interested in the welfare of their clients. They will provide a vigorous defense against the charges, for they would be poor attorneys if they did not. But many take the attitude of one, who stated to the author, "Look, I don't want to know if he is guilty or not. He is entitled to the best defense possible under the law, and I will do everything in my power to provide him with one. But I do feel he and his family need help, and I hope you can work with them." The professional should never attempt to compromise the functions of either the defense or the prosecuting attorney. They are sworn to play out certain roles in the legal drama and should not make exceptions or exclusions at the request of a therapist.

The judge too, plays an important role, although it is probably less crucial than that of the prosecutor, who is the one who decides whether charges will be brought. Judges are humans with personal biases and opinions, and many are fathers and mothers. The professional must always be mindful of the judge's responsibility to the abuser and to the members of the triad. The professional should never provide the judge with confidential material in chambers without prior clearance from the person involved.

The Sexual History

Sex abuse has as its primary symptom sexual behavior. In order to treat the problem, one must understand the symptom and its meaning. It is therefore necessary to obtain the sexual history of the adult male and adult female, and depending on the child's age and the circumstances of the complaint, the child's history as well.

It should be explained to those in the sexual abuse situation that obtaining sexual history is a normal and necessary part of the treatment process. They should be assured that the information will be confidential and that it is needed so that the professional can better understand and work with the persons involved. It cannot be stressed too strongly that the purpose is to help, not harm, the individual.

There are a number of sexual history, inventory, and data gathering forms and schedules available. Probably the most exhaustive was the one developed by Benjamin Karpman (1954), and many professionals have taken this sexual inventory form and modified it for their own purposes.

At the very least, the therapist should obtain information in the following areas:

1. Current complaint. Exactly what type of sexual abuse occurred. What were the circumstances and factors leading up to the event? Past history of sexual abuse with victim or other children.

Duration, frequency, and types of sexual activity. Feelings of all members of the triad over the event and subsequent complaint.

2. Past sexual history of each member involved. Age each was first aware of sexuality. First sexual experience: type and feelings. All sexual experiences: numbers, types, individuals involved. Nature and type of early marital sexual experiences. Nature and type of continuing sexual relationship.

3. Relationship between members of the triad.

4. Relationships with other family members.

Again, the sexual abuse is symptomatic of a disruption in relationships, particularly between the adults. Sex seems to be a type of barometer in marriage, and by charting the ups and downs of activities and feelings during the marriage, the therapist can judge the duration of disruption in the family. In some instances, particularly with the pansexual abuser, frequent and continued sexual activity is noted prior to, during, and after the abuse. But, it is not at all uncommon to find that the adults in the triad have not been sexually involved with each other for over a year.

In the area of family relationships there are a number of instruments that have been developed to assist therapists, and of course most therapists quickly develop their own indices that seem to be helpful to them. A form developed by Groezinger (1974) combines material on both the sexual and familial aspects of marriage. Groezinger developed her form after surveying existing ones in the areas of marriage counseling and sexual deviation. The form focuses on the adult members of the triad and can serve as a general guide for counselors and workers with limited experience in the field of sexual abuse.

Another useful inventory can be obtained from lists made by each individual member of the triad. They can be asked to write down the things they like, the things they dislike, what they like in other members of the triad, and what they dislike about other members of the triad. Each one can also be asked to list the strengths and weaknesses he or she perceives in the family unit. This material can be very useful to the therapist in learning about the individual perceptions of each person, particularly if the contents are discussed in a group, with all members of the triad present.

The beginning professional in child abuse is often surprised to find that the persons in the abuse situation know so little about each other and their likes and dislikes. In many respects they may strike the interviewer as virtual strangers living under the same roof, but this initial impression may reflect their lack of knowledge about one another rather than their lack of feeling. Sometimes, they know very little about themselves and their own interests, much less anyone else's. Many will impress the interviewer as uninterested and apathetic, but they are usually anything but that. One component that is hidden much of the time early in the therapeutic relationship is the anger that the adults have for each other. Much of the time the anger is diffuse and not recognized, and frequently it is vigorously denied. Nevertheless, it is present and will eventually be expressed with therapeutic assistance.

Successful therapy involves maintaining an active relationship with the abuser, spouse, and child. The traditional 50-minute appointment once or twice a month is ineffective. With that sort of schedule, the first to fail to keep an appointment will be the abuser, a month or two later the spouse will not appear, and lastly the child will stop coming.

In order to achieve some measure of success, it is beneficial to involve each in "work" in preparation for the next session. This may involve keeping a daily diary, writing autobiographical material, making notations on early marital experiences that were pleasant or unpleasant, and noting feelings and changes in family interaction during therapy. It is also important for the patients to achieve some sort of therapeutic success, or positive reinforcement, for their efforts. This may consist of reviewing their handling of certain situations, material, and communications before therapy was started. If the abuser or the others involved do not see any progress or tangible results for their time, money, and effort, they tend to drop out; that is why positive reinforcements are so necessary.

Long-Range Treatment of Sexual Abuse

The relationships between the professional and each member of the triad must be based on the interactions of two humans. People will not divulge information they feel guilty about to a person they do not trust and to whom they cannot relate in human terms. All too often, defensive persons have approached the abuser with the attitude that the abuser is inferior and the professional is superior. As one abuser related. "That social worker just looked at me and said, 'I've been trained to accept all kinds of behavior. Tell me about your perversions!' "

The relationship does not imply acceptance of the behavior but of the person. One of the most effective approaches is to be completely open and simply state, "I'm having difficulty in understanding how this occurred. Help me understand." Given the opportunity, most people will indeed help the professional to understand because they want to be understood and accepted. Members of the triad will know, regardless of any verbal assurances, how the professional really feels by picking up nonverbal cues. And there is nothing wrong in being human and acknowledging that discussing sex is uncomfortable for the members of the triad and the professional, if one is uncomfortable in this area.

A major problem in treating sexual abuse is the use of sexual terms. While professionals may feel comfortable using words such as coitus, fellatio, and cunnilingus, most of the people we work with in sexual abuse do not. With encouragement and warm support, patients will confide in the professional, but they will use the terms they are familiar with. It is incumbent on the professional to use those terms in discussion, even if they are "street words" often considered vulgar, since in many instances these are the only terms the patients know. Sometimes, professionals will "educate and manipulate" patients into using terms that are more comfortable for them.

To understand completely, it is sometimes necessary to know in some detail exactly what the client is stating. In one instance, a very young girl complained about "Daddy [her stepfather] sticking his 'ting' " in her. No damage was evident, and the matter was about to be dismissed when a social worker asked, "What 'ting'?" The child replied, "The 'ting' in his mouth," pointing to her tongue. Young children will also say that a person was "playing" with them. It is necessary to determine through gentle and supportive questioning what they mean.

With adults, it is also necessary to get some idea of what they feel is "normal" and acceptable behavior and what is "abnormal" and unacceptable. Many times, a general discussion of values and of what someone feels is "right and wrong" will be of great help in understanding that person.

For the sake of efficiency, it is easier to work with sexual abuse if there are two therapists, one working with the adults, the other with the children. Some therapists are more effective with adults and prefer working with them, and some prefer working with children and are highly effective in this regard. A few, of course, prefer working with the entire family. When two or more therapists are involved, they must hold regularly scheduled weekly consultations in order to coordinate their professional efforts. It is also mandatory that all the therapists working on the case be present when all members of the triad come together to talk through their problems.

Team therapy is not without its pitfalls and hazards, however, and if two therapists are involved they must respect and like each other professionally as well as personally. Honest differences of opinion will exist between competent professionals, but they should arrive at some middle ground, in order to present a united front to the patients. This front must be real, not artificial, and the therapists must accept the agreement emotionally as well as intellectually. Unless the situation is highly unusual, it is generally ill advised for the team to consist of a therapist or caseworker and a supervisor.

The Supervisory Relationship

Serving as a consultant, the author has met several hundred supervisors of staff working with physical and sexual abusers. Nearly all have said, with pride, something to this effect: "There is nothing my people cannot discuss with me. I'm very open and receptive, and

I try to be helpful." And around a thousand workers in the field, almost without exception, have vehemently disagreed in private with that statement.

Most beginning professionals are young and inexperienced. Many maintain a life style that is completely different from the middle-class climate of the office setting. Many have experimented with and/or used drugs. With some, marijuana is a commonplace experience. Many view their jobs as a community service tour of duty and have a deep commitment to the people of this country. Most have high ideals, principles, and integrity. They are effective not because of their vast training but because they like and care about other human beings, and this feeling comes through to the people with whom they are working.

Supervisors usually have several years of experience behind them, along with a master's degree, usually in social work. Most come from a middle-class background, are married, and have children in school. Most are five to fifty years older than the people they supervise. Many are fearful of drugs and do not understand life styles that differ from their own, such as unmarried couples living together. Most of them view their jobs as a profession, and the majority are removed from day-to-day contact with the people the agency serves. Like the beginning professionals, most supervisors are people of integrity, with high ideals and principles. Almost universally they demand far more of themselves than of those they supervise.

An information and communications gap generally exists between the supervisor and the supervisee. The relationship is authoritarian in nature: The supervisor writes the probationary evaluation and can determine for the most part whether or not the employee will continue with the agency. Consequently, many beginning professionals wish to appear in the best possible light and avoid discussing controversial issues with their supervisors. Further, they do not wish to alienate the "hand that feeds them"—in this case the taxpayer/agency/supervisor. Several illustrations of the communications gap come to mind from the author's experiences as a consultant:

After meeting with supervisory staff for three hours, assurances were given that while drugs were a real problem in the community, none of the staff of the agency "would think of using them." That evening, at a party given by workers of the agency, the question was asked, "A lot of people offer us 'dope.' Do you think it would help our relationship if we went ahead and smoked with them?"

A supervisor described one sexual abuser as having "uncontrolled sexual impulses. He had had relations with several women in addition to his wife." The professional working with the abuser was, unbeknownst to his supervisor, living with two females in a group arrangement satisfactory to all.

One sexual abuser was described as having "confused sexual identity" (because he was bisexual) by a supervisor. The professional working on the case admitted in confidence that she is homosexual, a fact not known to her supervisor.

One worker confided that he could not communicate with his supervisor. The worker was an active member of a fundamentalist religious sect. The supervisor acknowledged the communications gap, stating, "As an atheist, I just can't understand someone like him."

This gap has serious implications in the treatment of sexual abuse. More often than not, the supervisor will exercise supervisory guidance and power based on his or her own biases and sexual values. The professional actively working with the case may have completely different values, and the members of the triad may subscribe to a third and sometimes a fourth or fifth set. But these differences are never discussed, partly because professionals are reluctant to express their personal feelings and experiences as a way of facilitating communications and understanding.

Traditionally, supervisors have been promoted because of their experience in working with people and their seniority. But now it is time, at least in the treatment of abuse, to recognize that the person occupying the supervisory position might not be the best one to consult with and to supervise the individual case. Many supervisors have had little or no experience with abuse, particularly sexual abuse.

A satisfactory resolution may be to allow supervisors to maintain their responsibilities in seeing that forms and paperwork be completed but to turn therapeutic problems over to two or more professionals who are directly involved with abuse cases. In an agency in which there are five employees handling abuse cases, it would probably be more beneficial for those five to consult with each other and talk through their problems as equals than for each one to consult with the supervisor. In many areas professionals are already consulting with each other informally over coffee or lunch. It is but a short step to the outright recognition of the value of this practice.

Another reason for changing the professional consultation procedure, particularly in treating sexual abuse, is that movement and "eddy currents" can occur within a triad. If two professionals are involved with a family, in spite of theory, they are more attuned to what is transpiring than a supervisor who is not.

The Anger Component in Sexual Abuse

It has been suggested that the sexual abuse of a child by a father is the ultimate act of anger toward the wife. It repudiates her validity and worth as a person, a wife, and as a mother. For the successful treatment of sexual abuse it is necessary to determine with the abuser and the spouse where this anger arose, how it evolved and developed, and how it culminated in the event that was reported.

Many husbands are angry with their wives but do not become sexually involved with their daughters. Similarly, many wives are angry with their husbands, but do not become involved with their sons. Why, then, does sexual abuse occur? The psychological make-up of the participants, the family atmosphere, and, in many instances, environmental or situational factors all contribute to the genesis of sexual abuse.

The typical history of a sexually abusive man shows that upon marriage his wife expressed a massive dependency on him and made many demands for goods, services, and indicators of "a better way of life." Fulfilling these desires met the husband's initial needs and partly explains the attraction between the two. Many of these men work sixteen to eighteen hours a day and hold two jobs so that they can furnish a house and buy the latest appliances.

The wife usually becomes pregnant immediately after marriage and finds fulfillment in her role as a mother. The need for money increases. In addition, the wife is dependent in a number of other obvious ways; e.g., in many cases she does not drive an automobile and must be transported by the husband to the grocery store or to the doctor's office. Also, many wives are considered "good mothers but poor homemakers."

In many of these early marital situations, it almost seems as though a father-daughter relationship exists, with the male "protecting" the female from the onslaughts of life and the female enjoying this "protection." With the passage of time and the changing of roles, this situation becomes less meaningful and less rewarding to the male. Mild resentment is followed by anger toward the spouse (and frequently toward himself), but this anger is never discussed. Many sexually abusive fathers have made statements to the effect that "I made my bed and must lie in it."

The relationship between husband and wife deteriorates, yet their problems are not discussed or recognized. Outside influences buoy up the formal and legal maintainance of the marriage, which for all human intents and purposes is dead. These extraneous supports to the family are often the church, employment, and the extended family of one or both spouses.

The father seethes with anger and then becomes quite considerate of his children, replicating the early marriage pattern of caring for the helpless child and "protecting her from the world." In many cases he will expect great things of the children in every aspect of their life—e.g., helpfulness around the home, good grades in school, participation in church activities—and demand that they be neatly dressed and behave appropriately in public. This control extends, of course, to the selection of playmates, attendance at activities outside the home, and dating.

Frequently, everyone is shocked when sexual abuse is discovered. People will point out how well the father controlled the children and what a good person and strong man he is and was. Shortly afterwards this picture is turned into the despot-tyrant image of the sexual abuser. Finally, if the father did not permit the daughter to date or to be around boys, he is viewed as jealous and possessive. This model or explanation is highly suspect in view of the backgrounds of many abusers, for they are simply repeating other, earlier roles.

Therapy, then, becomes a process of reconstructing the source of anger, examining each parent's needs, finding the reasons for those needs, and seeing how the early marital relationship developed over the years and was replicated in the relationship with the children. Finally, it may include a partial reconstruction of the personalities of both adults and assistance to the child in sorting through the problem.

These parents stay together over the years because of massive, overwhelming, and somewhat unhealthy needs. The anger sometimes becomes the dominant force in the family. When the parents recognize the anger, express it, and realize why they have remained together, many of them separate or get divorced.

Knowing a little about the dynamics of such a family, we can now understand why the remedies that are sometimes offered are ineffective. Some suggested solutions have been, "Go on a second honeymoon and rediscover each other"; "Quit your second job"; "Learn how to drive"; "Go to church"; "Go to school"; "Get interested in [nonsexual] family activities and hobbies." These changes are in outward behavior or appearance, not in dynamics or structure, and unless the basic problems are resolved, the basic situation will remain. "Pull-yourself-up-by-your-bootstraps" suggestions sound nice, but, emotionally, the sexually abusive triad lacks bootstraps.

Precisely because the task of therapy for sexual abusers is so difficult it must be handled by specialists in the field. These cases should be treated at a mental health clinic that is willing to work intensively with the triad or at a public agency where the professionals have small caseloads and specialize in sexual abuse; or they should be referred to a private practitioner. Therapy involves discomfort if not pain, for the individual is being called upon to go through a process of change to a point at which mechanisms that have served a psychological purpose for a lifetime are no longer needed.

Many abusers will willingly attempt short-range behavior changes as a solution to the problem, but they are ineffective. Their use is analogous to having a person with a drinking problem switch from one alcoholic beverage to another in an attempt to control consumption. This is not to say that changes will not evolve, but the outward changes in behavior must be the result of changes from within.

Sometimes environmental or situational manipulation becomes the treatment of choice from a patient or cost point of view. For example, if a 9-year-old and a 6-year-old are sleeping in one bedroom and a 14-year-old girl who has been sexually abused by her father is sleeping in another, it behooves us to suggest a change in the sleeping arrangements. Two actual cases illustrate how these manipulations can work:

Ann, 16 years old, had been sexually involved with her father for four years. In three months Ann would finish high school. It was arranged that she would attend the university, beginning with summer school, with financial support from her parents and her grandfather.

Mabel, 14 years old, had been involved sexually with her stepfather at least twice. Her stepfather and her mother expressed no interest in treatment and actively resisted efforts to involve them. Mabel's aunt (her natural father's sister) asked that Mabel be placed with her permanently.

In both instances, it would have been folly to attempt long-range treatment of the adults. Rather, the effort was focused on the girls, to assist them in working through their feelings. Other suggestions in other households are: temporary removal of the abuser, temporary removal of the child, taking all the children shopping rather than leaving one girl with the father, insisting that the mother and father shop together, changing jobs and job shifts so that the father is not left home for eight hours with a daughter. These will not "solve" the abuse, of course, for it is only a symptom of deeper problems.

The Mentally Ill Sexual Abuser

The mentally ill sexual abuser of children is often the one who comes to public attention and is the one who causes great anxiety among the general public, but this type is rare, and fortunately so. The sexual abuse is only a symptom of the underlying pathology or illness. Mentally ill abusers should probably be institutionalized for treatment for their own protection as well as that of the children.

The difficulty in treating mentally ill sexual abusers is that they have committed a criminal act or come under quasi-criminal laws that make treatment difficult if not impossible. Prisons maintain, understandably, that they are understaffed and are not capable of providing the treatment necessary for the sex offender who is involved with children. On the other hand, mental hospitals often take the position that the mentally ill sexual abuser is a dangerous criminal and needs to be in prison rather than in a mental hospital. Historically, as a result of the difficulties experienced with this type of individual, two middle-ground approaches have been used, neither of which has proved satisfactory.

One approach has been to construct mental health facilities (psychiatric wards) in prisons and to construct prison units in mental hospitals (security wards). The prison setting does not lend itself to treatment even if it takes place in a psychiatric ward, nor does the hospital security building. The net result has been that the mentally ill sexual abuser lives in a therapeutic never-never land.

The second approach has resulted in the enactment of "CSP," or criminal sexual psychopath laws, in twenty-nine states. The term *psychopath* or *sociopath* connotes a "sick mind" or a type of mental illness, but it also constitutes a moral or behavior judgment. Long ago Dr. William White called psychopathy "the wastebasket of psychiatry," yet the term has taken on increased importance in connection with sexual crimes. Because of the public hue and cry, the criminal sexual psychopath laws are broad and allow great discretion. In some states the court may convene on its own and make a postconviction determination of sexual psychopathy. Procedural safeguards are in many instances lacking, and the offender can be committed for an indefinite period of time, ranging from one day to life.

In addition to receiving little or nothing in the way of treatment, the offender cannot be released until someone is willing to affirm that he has been "cured" and will not repeat his behavior. Few professionals are willing to make such a statement, since no one can guarantee another's behavior.

The Sexually Abusive Stepfather

When a stepfather enters a home, he is for all intents and purposes a stranger who is attempting to assume a new role as father and husband. With very young children this transition is not too difficult, but as the children get older the assertion of authority and integration into the family becomes more difficult.

With teen-agers, the assumption of the stepfather role can result in severe difficulties, particularly with a boy who has been the only male in the home for any length of time. With teen-age girls, discipline can become a real arena of conflict. The difficulties the stepfather entering the home experiences in being accepted can lead to sexual abuse.

Many stepfathers enter the home in their late twenties or thirties and are faced with a teen-age girl. Feeling uncomfortable in becoming an "instant father," they rely on comfortable measures of coping with women: They seduce them with words and actions. The stepfather "woos over" his teen-age stepdaughter and develops a real attraction for her, which, coupled with the situation of living under the same roof, can result in sexual relations.

There is another side to this coin, and that is the teen-age daughter. She is feeling her sexuality and beginning to see herself as a sexual human being. In trying out her attractiveness to adults of the opposite sex, she can be very seductive and highly competitive with the mother for the attentions of the new handsome stranger in the home.

A third factor is the mother. In physical abuse we have noted cases in which the mother, because of her intense personal need, has permitted the abuse of her children under the guise of permitting the stepfather entry into the home as a father. Similarly, in sexual abuse of children, because of her psychological needs, the mother sometimes permits her daughter to be sexually abused in order to "keep the stepfather." The daughter then becomes an added inducement for the stepfather, so that the mother will not "lose" her husband.

Future Treatment Programs and Strategies in Sexual Abuse

Short-Range Goals. We must first recognize that the problem does in fact exist and that sexual abuse is substantively different from physical abuse. We must recognize that treatment is a fairly difficult, intensive experience that changes the family basically.

We can hasten part of the therapeutic process by requesting a speedy disposition of the legal charges against the suspected abuser and work toward assuring the confidentiality of any information given in a professional relationship. If professional help is started immediately, arrangements must be made to keep the professional from being subpoenaed into court to testify for or against the patient in a criminal action.

In the current state of the art, most public agencies dealing with abuse should, through referral or purchase-of-services, contract and/or refer out most cases of sexual abuse to professionals and agencies capable of providing the requisite professional services and of seeing the members of the triad on an intensive basis. In those situations where the professional staff is available but the time for intensive services is not, the community should be informed, and it should be explained why the agency is unable to meet the problem of sexual abuse from a treatment standpoint.

For teen-age girls, placement out of the home with interested relatives may be a satisfactory and efficient solution to the long-standing family problems that resulted in the sexual involvement. This does not alter the family dynamics; it only removes the child from the source of the abuse. In these instances, primary efforts should be directed to the victim of the abuse.

At the national level, we should begin collecting information on the successful and unsuccessful cases with which agencies and private practitioners in the fields of psychology, psychiatry, law, medicine, nursing, and social work have come in contact since 1970. We need computerized data that will provide insights, and we desperately need data on the adult female who sexually abuses a male child. These efforts should begin immediately.

Long-Range Goals. We should begin thinking about developing a cadre of professionals in public agencies charged with investigating and treating physical and sexual abuse of children, who can provide treatment at the local level in every community. This force of professionals should be assisted through specialized in-service training to develop expertise in the area, particularly in sexual abuse.

Universities should be encouraged through grants to develop specialized courses in the treatment of child abuse and to provide graduate-level training in the treatment of sexual abuse.

Treatment of sexual abuse (as well as physical abuse) must be exempted from caseload ratios of traditional public welfare agencies. A caseload of 50, 100, or 150 in the field of abuse, with forms to fill out and reports to write, is simply ridiculous.

Different and innovative treatment strategies should be explored as alternatives to our cumbersome, expensive, and difficult way of treating sexual abusers. Behavior modification, for example, may offer promise in a limited manner. Currently, one of our main problems is the lack of motivation to undergo a long, painful, and expensive process. The major motivation of a large number of abusers is directly proportionate to the legal threat to the abuser. We must explore additional ways of obtaining treatment leverage in sexual abuse, so that whatever treatment is used can be effective.

We must change the legal status of children and elevate their civil rights to the level of adults'. We must recognize their worth, validity, and rights to the degree where the burden of proof in sexual abuse is no longer placed on them. In part, this will be accomplished through public education, and in part it is a problem to which legal scholars must address themselves. Let us hope that an organization such as the American Civil Liberties Union will one day press for change in this area.

Finally, we must recognize that mentally ill sexual abusers of children do not receive treatment, and many times they are released only after long years of incarceration. We must develop entirely new means of treating this disturbed group.

In the long-range treatment planning, we must avoid the "gimmicks" that offer quick and easy solutions to very complex situations. Federal authorities, most of all, must avoid this trap in funding child abuse programs. The prospect looks attractive, there is a good press, and a little talk is stirred up when Senator Foghorn announces that HEW has given $200,000 for a Neighborhood Child Abuse Prevention Program. But the program consists of neighbors' calling each other or teachers' asking children if their fathers molested them. The ultimate answer to sexual abuse and its treatment will take years of basic research with carefully controlled studies, and it will be difficult and expensive.

CHAPTER TEN

Abused Children: Observations and Comments

Literally thousands of books and articles have been written on children. Serious students of child psychology have at their disposal a vast literature dealing with child development, child rearing, children's behavior—both normal and abnormal, and treatment. It is not necessary to review the varying approaches, but some words are in order about abused children and treatment that attempts to resolve the abuse. These comments are not based on statistics, but personal notations made in working with children who have been physically or sexually abused. As such, these remarks will agree with the views of some writers in the field and disagree with those of others. This is quite understandable, for some cases have greater impact and influence than others and people working with abused children will form impressions based on their own experiences. Certain common threads appear in the treatment of the adult abuser, and similar common elements arise in working with the abused child. Likewise, it is important to note the vast differences that can exist in treatment.

It is first necessary to understand the role of children in America, which was discussed earlier. Most children feel at the mercy of adults, and most are in fact dependent on the adults around them, whether the adult is motivated to help or harm the child. Children's contacts with adults are fairly restricted and highly ritualized. The most significant adults in their lives are their parents or adult caretakers, one or more of whom may be the abuser with whom we are dealing. Children are sometimes exposed to other adults in times of stress. Often abused children associate doctors and nurses with pain and are fearful of what will be inflicted on them by medical personnel, regardless of their humane motivation. At school, other meaningful adults enter their lives, and they have to share a teacher with twenty-five to forty other children. Some abused children have been in contact with many adults (such as their mothers' boyfriends or their fathers' girlfriends) who pose varying degrees of physical and psychological threat. The physical threat is real, and the psychological threat of sharing a parent with another adult (e.g., a stepparent) is often difficult for a child to handle. Other adults with whom they come in contact may be grandparents, who may or may not be as harsh as the parents, and assorted aunts, uncles, or other relatives.

Professionals working in the field of child abuse must be honest with themselves about what type of patient—adult or child—they prefer and are more effective with. Rarely does one find a professional who is equally at ease and competent with adults and children. For this reason, among others, it is usually preferable to have one professional working with the adults in an abuse situation and another working with the child or children. The sex of the therapist makes no demonstrable difference in the effectiveness of the treatment of either children or adults, nor does the therapist's age or race. There may be a transient reaction to these attributes, but it fades away as the relationship with the therapist develops. Children rapidly relate to the *person* they are working with, not their physical makeup.

The first rule in treating children is to recognize that they are not miniature adults. Their physical and psychological development and their innate capabilities will vary. They also have different needs than adults and react differently. It may sound trite to mention the fact, but it cannot be emphasized too much that all children are not alike. In fact, two children from the same family can be poles apart in their views, personality, and actions. This emphasis is needed because frequently a professional will refer to "the Smith children" rather than "John and Mary." The former appellation does not recognize the children as individuals. Too often treatment is given to "the Smith children" as a group, rather than individually. It is relatively harmless to assume that all the Smith children like chocolate ice cream when one dislikes it, but it can be a therapeutic disaster to assume that all the Smith children love their mother when one hates her with a passion.

At the first contact with an abused child, professionals tend to expect too much both from themselves and from the child. They look for instant rapport, particularly when the professional appears in the role of the child's "savior." Unfortunately, the child neither realizes nor accepts this fact. If the child is hospitalized, he or she is probably experiencing pain or its aftermath and is often frightened, confused, and fearful, regardless of exterior appearances. It is simply unrealistic to expect that the child will relate instantly to a stranger and will seek long-term comfort from that contact. Most children do not have such discriminatory powers. When a child is under this type of duress, it is best if the professional who will be working with the situation is available and can be seen by the child, and that he or she interact in a supportive, nonthreatening manner.

If the first contact is in the home, it is best to focus one's attention and interaction on the adults. This gives the child an opportunity to observe the professional unobtrusively, to form judgments, and to weigh the situation. This arrangement is ideal but it is often unworkable, particularly if damages are obvious or if the abuser will not leave the home temporarily and the child must be removed for his or her own protection.

More often than not, the abused child feels he or she did something wrong, feels guilty about causing harm, discomfort, and embarrassment to the adult caretaker, and will frequently try to protect the abuser by manufacturing explanations for the injuries without prompting by the abuser. Many simply rely on techniques they have learned that minimize abuse: They shy away from contact and are nonverbal to the point of either being mute or responding in monosyllables.

Sometimes, there is a complete reversal from this usual pattern, and the abused child will reach out to anyone. Although it is hard for some professionals to accept, some abused children will actually go to anyone who beckons them. This has led some unknowing professionals to rule out abuse on the assumptions that the child could not have been abused because he or she is so "lovable," or that if the child had been abused he or she would avoid contact with anyone. Both assumptions are false.

The purely medical aspects of abused children pose unconscious problems in treatment. The scars, bruises, burns, or casts that are the result of abuse can generate feelings of anger and hostility in the adults involved and can cause the professional to identify with the child. Both influences interfere with the overall therapeutic effort. Further, the child can often sense the professional's unexpressed anger toward the parent, which in turn causes the child to become protective of the parent and draw away from the therapist. Obviously, sensitive professionals cannot be indifferent to the damage inflicted on children, but they can constantly monitor themselves and their feelings. Supervisors and coworkers can be of invaluable assistance in helping them be aware of these feelings.

In addition to the purely physical damage, abused children seem to differ from their nonabused peers in that they often have multiple physical problems. Most experience developmental difficulties. It is not uncommon for them to be small for their age, a determination that can be made objectively by using the Boston Anthropometric Scale. Frequently, they will have medical problems or physical defects from past injuries or abuse. In several cases, the author has been aware of central nervous system defects, which probably arose from injuries to the head. Finally, a seemingly disproportionate number of abused children have speech defects. These observations from clinical contact are borne out to some extent in Elmer and Gregg (1967).

The physical underdevelopment and the speech defects are thought-provoking. Is there some genetic factor that causes abused children to be smaller than their peers? Is their size due to deprivation, the abuse itself, or are they—in the analytic sense—acting out and fulfilling their parents' wishes that they do not exist? We do not know at this point, and additional research is needed. Similarly, why is it so many seem to have speech defects? Is the causation organic, psychological, damage, or a combination of factors? Again, we simply do not know.

These physical problems affect the treatment of abused children, and none are therapeutic assets. Often, the treatment must be reduced to the most basic level or the primary effort must be redirected to the parent. This is not to say that handicapped children do not have feelings; they do, but it can be difficult for them to express themselves and it is sometimes difficult to understand them. These observations on physically abused children do not apply to sexually abused children.

Of course, no treatment that involves verbal communication can be given to very young children or infants. They simply cannot discuss their feelings if they cannot talk, and this is exactly the situation with many infants and young children who are abused. Again, the primary effort must be toward the adults. Even though we cannot offer treatment that demands verbal interaction, we cannot overlook the child, for there is one basic principle every professional working in abuse should know and apply: The younger the child the more lethal the situation and the more necessary it is to invoke the protective function of the law.

If an adult man weighing 180 pounds struck another man of the same size, the victim might be knocked off balance. If the same adult struck a 12-year-old with the same force, he might break the child's nose. If the child is 6, the blow might knock him unconscious and perhaps cause injuries when the child struck the floor. A one-year-old child struck with the same amount of force will most likely be killed, and if only six weeks old, the child will certainly die.

A "breaking point" occurs when a child can crawl, another when it can walk, and a third when it can run away from the abuser. An infant is truly helpless, immobile, and extremely vulnerable in a crib. Either the abuser or the infant must leave the home temporarily when we begin to work with the situation. Even if there is only the suspicion of abuse, when it concerns an infant it is better to err on the side of protecting the child.

Abused children, as we have noted, often feel guilty about

directing attention toward their parents or adult caretakers. They may be defensive and may generate explanations of how the injuries might have occurred in an accidental manner. Perhaps it is for these reasons that abused children usually take longer than nonabused children to develop a meaningful and trusting relationship with an outsider. On the whole they are quite defensive (particularly as they become older) and cautious in commiting themselves to a relationship in which they must discuss their feelings about parents and parent-child interaction.

On the other hand, physically abused children seem to have two advantages over other children: Once they do begin to invest their feelings in a relationship with a professional they are capable of doing so very rapidly and completely; and they seem to follow through diligently on any planning, behavior, or action that is mutually agreed upon.

A therapeutic problem that is little discussed but which certainly has bearing on the treatment plan is the great number of professionals that a child may come in contact with over a short span of time. Within a 72-hour period he or she may encounter physicians and nurses, the police, an investigative worker, an intake worker, a foster care specialist, foster parents, and the person with whom the child will have continuing contact. Although the child is in contact with most of these people for only a short time, they all expect some investment of feeling, yet they pass the child from one to another in a rather cavalier manner. This practice constitutes agency abuse of a child, and it is the antithesis of sound treatment planning. It is no wonder that many abused children become nonverbal and have problems in relating to professionals.

In dealing with abused children, experience proves that it is best to inform them in advance of any treatment plans, particularly if they are to be placed outside the home. The foster care should be discussed in considerable detail with the child. It is also wise for foster parents not to try to approach the child quickly or to expect an immediate response from the child. Rather, the child should be permitted to move and relate at his or her own speed. We must remember that the abuse many of these children have suffered resulted from an adult caretaker's anger at their behavior. Often they had not been told what was expected of them. For this reason abused children placed in foster care need to know in advance specifically what is expected of them: What they may and may not do, mealtimes, bedtime, and the many other little things that add up to a major part of their functioning in a foster home. Children who can read can often benefit from a written statement, and this statement should also explain the rewards or benefits that they will enjoy.

Children need to know the truth and to be prepared for the consequences and implications of reality. It is unwise to say that life in a foster home will be "better," for the abused child knows it will not. It is unwise to say that the placement will not last more than "a few days," under the mistaken notion that such a statement will relieve temporary separation anxiety if the placement will be lengthy. And children can accept truth and changing situations. In a case on which the author worked, the placement of the victimized child was not to exceed three days, during which time the abusive father was supposed to move out temporarily. He decided not to, and it was the author's responsibility to tell the child he would have to remain in the foster home for a longer time.

I simply said, "I told you a lie but I didn't mean to. I thought you would be back home in three days but we can't work it out. You may have to stay here for some time while I work with your Mom and Dad." The boy responded, "Did you know that when we talked about it yesterday?" "No," I said. "As a matter of fact I thought you would be home by tomorrow." He replied, "Well, it ain't a lie 'cause you didn't know beforehand." When the child returned home some three weeks later, he said, "I'm glad you said you told me a lie even though you didn't, and didn't mean to. I knew sooner or later you would get me back home." This particular incident points up the fact that children can usually accept or learn to live with reality if they are told the truth. They cannot abide shams, half-truths, and misleading statements designed to "protect" them, which end up being more devastating than the reality with which they must cope.

Communications is a trite, hackneyed word, but however offensive it is, it must be discussed as it relates to abused children. To treat a verbal child effectively, we must use words that are meaningful to that child. With a 16-year-old sexually abused girl, one can often talk on an adult, or nearly adult, level. But if the abused child is only 2, its vocabulary is limited, and words may have completely different meanings to the child than to the therapist. Abstractions and philosophical ideas are simply beyond the comprehension of very young children, and one must use concrete, specific, and reality-oriented words that they can understand. If *you* do not understand what a child means, or is attempting to say, ask. And if it is necessary to ask for an interpretation, it should be done in a warm, supporting way rather than in a threatening manner. The child has good reason to be fearful and to withdraw if an adult is "offended" or quizzical.

When abused children make a shift in emotional commitment and invest feelings in their therapists, they will often become over-zealous in "winning them over." They will attempt to please and, to that end, will expand and expound on any subject that generates the adults' interest. This is normal and natural, and even when children distort the truth, they are doing so only because of a need for acceptance, respect, and love. This behavior is indicative of short-comings in the treater as well as the treated, for the focus should not be on the needs of the therapist, but on those of the child.

Frequently abused children are described by caseworkers foster parents, psychiatrists, and psychologists as untruthful or manipulative because of the reckless abandon with which they interpret certain events. Rarely is this the case; in most instances they are simply struggling with a new relationship and a new figure in whom they have a considerable emotional investment. This is a crucial point for both the child and the therapist. While it is gratifying to have a child invest such a degree of feeling in an adult that he or she will say anything to gain acceptance (which the child equates with love), the situation can be damaging, for in almost all abuse situations, the primary figures should be the parents, not the therapists. A case could also be made that the negative label of "liar" applied to abused children merely reflects the professionals' awareness of the massive investment on the part of the children, which the professionals are not prepared to cope with and therefore reject the child through pejorative labeling. This explanation is admittedly speculative and bears additional investigation.

The work with the child must be related to the therapeutic efforts directed to the parent. The child should be attuned to the times of parental stress, need, or conditions conducive to abuse and should be helped to identify and alter behavior that may be disturbing to the parent. Later, the child's attention should be focused on his or her own needs and how they might be met by the parents, with help from the therapist. Initially, the child must make the accommodations in order to prevent further abuse, but eventually there should be a joint accommodation by the child and the parents, and more important, recognition of the child's rights and accommodations on the part of the parent to meet the child's needs.

A crucial point in the development of the family arises when the parent or adult abuser ceases employing physically brutal means of retaliation against the child. At this time the parent may be receiving support individually or in a group and may work diligently toward exploring nonabusive child-coping mechanisms. Unfortunately, many children are thus denied the only security and consistency they have known—physical punishment—and severely test the adult's intentions and new-found resolve. It is at this stage that they most need help, reassurance, support, and insight into the change that the entire family is undergoing. Rather than telling children "don't 'act out' at this time," they should be helped to see that they are central to the process, that changes are occurring because of them, and that they in turn must work toward change. In short, the accent must be placed on the positive contributions that the child can make.

Our task as individuals working with abused children is clear but extremely complex. On the one hand we need the relationship and investment of feeling by the child to achieve the desired movement. On the other hand, we must not allow the primary focus to rest with us rather than with the parents. The therapist must walk a difficult tightrope. Many discussions and conferences have centered on the question of whom we should opt for, the parent or the child. Most of these discussions are based on transference and countertransference, or the investment of feelings by the abuser, the abused, and the therapist(s). Such discussions are nonproductive and misdirected, for in "taking sides" we must not prefer either one or exclude either one. At all times we are working with a family unit, and our goal must be reintegration as a viable whole whenever possible. The therapist, not the abusive parent, should be the transitory figure in the abused child's life.

While the physically abused child is usually young and not uncommonly under a year old, the sexually abused child is much older. Cases of sexual abuse of very young infants are rare. Girls and boys appear in almost equal numbers among the physically abused, but girls predominate among the sexually abused. Although statistics are lacking, most sexually abused children are probably between 4 and 14 years of age.

In physical abuse, the stigma is attached or directed to the parent, and the child is viewed as the innocent victim. In sexual abuse this pattern is often reversed, and the abused girl is viewed with suspicion or mistrust, as though she may have contributed to her fate. The child who was once "pure" is now "tainted" with the curse of sexuality. There is also a morbid sort of curiosity on the part of many adults as to what transpired between the adult and the child, and this is much more obvious in sexual than in physical abuse.

For these reasons, sexually abused children probably need and can benefit by more support from professionals. It is not uncommon for the accused adult male to order the child out of the home until such time as she repents and retracts her accusation. The advocacy role of the professional must be very strong in working with the sexually abused child. The following case will illustrate the pressures a child may encounter:

Tuesday, noon: The sexual abuse of an 8-year-old girl, Julie, was reported to authorities by a maternal aunt, who suspected abuse.

Tuesday, 2 P.M.: Julie was seen in school by a worker of the local agency. Julie verified the sexual abuse by her stepfather. Several incidents had occurred over a period of three months.

Tuesday, 3:30 P.M.: Conference with mother and stepfather.

Abuse denied. Mother angry, accused Julie of being "chronic liar." Stepfather wanted Julie placed in mental institution. Insisted on her being out of home. Julie placed in foster care at 7 P.M. Author called as consultant at 9 P.M.

Wednesday, 8 A.M.: Julie in school.

Wednesday, 9 A.M.: Foster parents relate Julie cried herself to sleep. Foster mother told Julie it would "be good to talk about it and get all of it out." Julie refused.

Wednesday, 10 A.M.: Call from police department detectives who had heard about case and want to interview Julie.

Wednesday, 11 A.M.: Call from school counselor. She had attempted to "help" Julie and had "interviewed Julie for two hours helping her to express herself over this 'awful' thing." School counselor thinks Julie is "psychotic."

Wednesday, noon: Julie removed from school, taken to consultant's office, later placed in foster care home for afternoon after definite instructions were given to foster parents.

This brief account demonstrates the pressures that can be brought upon a sexually abused child in just twenty-four hours. She was seen by a worker whom she did not know and asked about a very anxiety-ridden matter, rejected by her mother and her stepfather, wrenched from her home and placed with two strangers, again talked to by a strange adult about the abuse, and grilled for two hours the following day by a school counselor. Compounding the situation was exposure to a strange man who would be working with her in the future. It is no wonder that the child was frightened and upset. The only ones who handled themselves professionally, it should be added, were the detectives, who said, "When you think she is ready, we would like to talk to her."

In situations such as this, the child must be told at the outset that she need not discuss the abuse with anyone but the therapist. The foster parents, school counselor, parents, and all other adults should be informed that the child has been instructed not to talk about it, and on occasion the author has given children typewritten notes to give adults if they try to pry into the matter. The note simply states that they have been instructed not to talk with anyone about the matter except the therapist, and if any questions arise the person reading the note may call the office and speak with the writer.

Not infrequently, someone will insist on a physical (primarily vaginal) examination of the child. One of three reasons are usually given: to determine the presence of semen, to determine if the hymen has been ruptured (which would show if she had been sexually abused in the past), and to determine if venereal disease is present. The first reason is legitimate if the alleged abuse occurred a short time before and the evidence is needed for criminal prosecution. The second reason is patently absurd, and the third is usually based on the assumption that if sex (an evil) is involved so must another evil (venereal disease) be present.

As a rule, all examinations should be opposed because criminal prosecution will not result unless a stranger is involved; even then, there will probably be no conviction. Children make poor witnesses in court, and the trauma of court appearances and cross-examination is usually more harmful than the abuse. In addition, the physical examination itself can be very traumatic for the child because she knows it is not a general one but is being performed for a specific reason. The exception to this rule is if the child complains, without prompting, of any pain, discharge, or bleeding, and at that time medical attention should be immediate. Reactions of girls to examinations vary widely. Some look forward to the examination because they believe it will enhance their credibility. Some actively resist the idea and become quite angry. Most, however, react the way our society dictates: They comply simply because an adult says it is necessary.

Some comment needs to be made about the girl of 14 or 15 who is deeply in love with her father, and he with her. Treatment in these cases is nearly impossible. Professionals often feel anger toward the father, and cannot understand that the girl would willingly be involved sexually with her father. One perceptive 16-year-old clarified the matter for the author when she stated, "John [her father] is my biological father, but not socially."

In this context, we can better understand the situation, and while we may speculate to no purpose how the denial of the social role arose, we cannot say these girls are "mentally ill." Coupled with a shift in the father's behavior is the daughter who is developing a sexual role in an adult society. All girls and boys go through a period in which they find out how attractive they are to members of the other sex. If we really "reach out" in trying to understand the girl in these situations, we can see how rewarding and reinforcing it must be for the girl. She is obviously wanted sexually, has an adult male lover, has a secret liaison, and is playing an adult female role. A therapist of a psychoanalytical bent would also point out that the girl in this situation has attained the normally unattainable—seduction of the father.

A sexually abused female involved in an incestuous relationship should always be offered future help. If a girl has been sexually involved with her father and later marries or takes up a long-term commitment with a young man, her family situation is quite different from the usual one, and premarital counseling is desired and indicated. The professional should always point out that she may return to the agency in the future and receive counseling.

Sexually abused boys and girls can frequently work through and express their feelings easily and quickly. Many are more traumatized by the societal response that followed than by the actual abuse. One incident that called for wholesale psychotherapy concerned four girls and three boys, all in the first and second grade, who were walking home from school. As they passed a garage in an alley, a man opened his coat and exposed his penis to the children. They continued home at a leisurely rate. One girl told her mother, who called the police. Several police cars entered the area searching for the now-departed "flasher." Fathers rushed home from work and grabbed weapons, searching the neighborhood. Ministers and neighbors hurried to several of the homes. When asked about their response to the man who exposed himself, the children said they giggled. None were traumatized, and they apparently accepted the event with good grace until the parents overreacted. The adults rather than the children could have profited from therapeutic intervention.

A few children are both physically and sexually abused. Although one can say that any damage or penetration constitutes physical injury, it is not in this context that we are speaking. Some abusers have not only involved children in sexual behavior but have also burned them with cigarettes or otherwise tortured them. Fortunately these cases are few and far between. Sadistic, and associating sexual pleasure with pain, these very ill men (who are often strangers) can cause great harm. When this occurs, children's minds frequently block out the horror, and with support they recover quickly. A few are permanently damaged physically and psychologically and require massive, long-term, coordinated treatment by an interdisciplinary team.

Some children who are abused incorporate the abusive measures into their own fulfillment:

Dr. J. is a 32-year-old dentist, "normal in all respects except one," by his own account. As a child his grandmother and grandfather would usually find something he had done wrong during the day, for which they would bind his hands over his head and tie him to the bedpost. This disciplinary measure was used on him from age 4 to 13, at which time his grandfather died and he went to live with a maternal aunt. He now finds, "The only way I can get a good night's sleep is to tie my hands to the bed." His reason for seeking professional help was, "While it doesn't bother me, it does bother my wife."

Mrs. A. was consistently given enemas for misbehavior as a child by her father, whom she says she "worshipped." Throughout her adult life she has experienced problems with bowel movements, and states that when she is depressed or anxious, "The best treatment is to give myself an enema."

Although some children do suffer long-term effects of physical and sexual abuse, it is surprising how rarely long-term damage of a psychological nature occurs. All children, abused and nonabused, are exposed to things in life that constitute hazards or traumas that should in theory affect them adversely but do not. Children are different from adults: They are resilient and pliable and accept with good grace things that would have a prolonged adverse effect on most adults. Children have self-healing mechanisms and protective devices that help them through difficult and traumatic situations. Abused children seem to be able to isolate and insulate certain aspects of the abuse. One of the functions of therapy or treatment should be to help these normal mechanisms do their work. Although we cannot prove their existence, most clinicians who have worked with abused children will attest to the presence of these mechanisms. Universally, however, one thing seems to remain with the physically abused child, and that is the utilization of violence as a means of solving problems. And so we know with certainty that today's abused child is tomorrow's abusive parent.

CHAPTER ELEVEN

Strategies for Change

We have examined the problem of physical and sexual abuse of children in America and have looked at ways of treating abuse situations. Throughout, we have stressed that the majority of abusers are not "sick" in the pathological sense, but rather reflect their own problems and child rearing in dealing with their children. It should come as no surprise that we are simply continuing an intergenerational tradition of harsh child-rearing practices. There is no real hope of a major decrease in child abuse unless we address ourselves to the matter of prevention. To do so we must change the patterns of child rearing in America, and this will require a major effort in research and public education.

Others have suggested that child abuse can be decreased if not eliminated through programs for the amelioration of poverty, substandard housing, and other negative social conditions. Educational efforts stress the pathological nature of abusers and the helplessness of children, some experts have suggested new roles for agencies, while others hope that present structures can meet the problem, and the current thrust in funding is for "experimental" programs. But these approaches, while honestly espoused, do little to alleviate or eradicate child abuse.

There is no doubt that the elimination of poverty would reduce the overall dimensions of the problem by relieving the situational pressures on some individuals. There is no doubt that substandard housing needs improvement and that every child needs protection from vermin and rats. And there is no question that a few pathological abusers do in fact need help through the traditional mental health approach. But these measures only touch on a few aspects of abuse and fail to meet the basic problem. In view of our cultural history and the status of our children, there can be no serious doubt that most abusers do not abuse their children because they are poor or because they are pathological. Continuing with this mode of thought will only result in failure to meet the basic issues.

Let us take a fresh view of the problem, in a manner that is comfortable and with which the reader is now familiar. Let us approach America and its child-rearing practices in the same manner in which we approach the abuser, through a therapeutic model that is not designed to assess blame or to punish but to help the patient improve.

Initially, when we call for the abolition of abuse everyone will agree with the goal. But when we tell American parents who flog, beat, spank, and switch children that this practice is wrong, we may expect the very same reaction we encounter in abuse situations: hostility, resistance, and anger. Parents with whom violence is central in child rearing will protest that they love their children and punish them physically for their best interests, will deny abuse, and will attack the person making the statement. Others will rush to their defense: ministers repeating biblical injunctions from Proverbs and politicians seeking reelection, particularly those politicians and ministers who employ violence on their own children, and some making dire predictions of increases in violent crime. We can also expect some mental health professionals to defend violence toward children on the grounds that it "assists in developing external controls," "gives needed structure to the child," or some other mistaken notion that is applied only to children. It is interesting to note that the use of violence is defended in child rearing, but it is rarely proposed for those populations where internal and external controls have demonstrably broken down, such as adult criminals or the mentally ill.

Our first goal must be to assist our "patient," in this case, America, in recognizing the need for help. Probably the most effective way to achieve it is to appeal to the country's concern for children. Most parents do in fact love their offspring and want better things for their children than for themselves. One of the strengths of this country is its willingness to try, to explore new methods, and to be open-minded about new ideas. From these traits arose our juvenile court system (which is truly an American invention), our extensive social service systems, and our advanced educational system. This same spirit may move us to attack the problem of child abuse.

Our overriding goal must be the elevation of children in American society and the observance of their rights.

Short-Range Goals

Children represent a significant portion of the American citizenry. They are of all colors, religions, socioeconomic classes, abilities, and hopes. They represent our greatest national resource, yet they are ignored and overlooked because they lack political leverage and representation. Many federal, state, and local agencies have programs designed for and geared to children but most of them are ineffective in representing children, elevating their status, and preventing or even treating child abuse.

At the federal level we have executive agencies and cabinet posts concerned with such aspects of American life as agriculture; commerce; housing; health, education, and welfare; treasury; interior; and defense. All of them express a concern for children, yet even in food issuance programs we see that the commodities issued bear little or no relation to the nutritional needs of Americans but are related to the surpluses generated by agribusiness.

We need nothing short of a cabinet-level agency concerned with children and their rights and well being. Toward this end we should dismantle many existing programs concerned with children and begin again with a new basic philosophy. This agency should not only concern itself with the health, education, and welfare of American children but also push aggressively for the recognition and protection of children and serve as their advocate. It should point out and work toward the elimination of programs that harm children, such as the commodities program. It should have its own legal arm.

This cabinet department would not require additional millions of dollars but could be created by reassigning and realigning federal personnel and programs and placing them under the aegis of one agency. Several short-range goals for this agency might be:

1. Evaluation of exactly what programs are offered for children, which are needed, which are not needed, and what needs of children are unmet and why.
2. Elimination of duplicative, outmoded, and timeworn efforts.
3. Coordination of existing programs.
4. Development of an advocacy role and a philosophy for the protection and development of children.

The creation of such a cabinet-level agency should not require more than five years, during which time these goals should be accomplished.

Another short-range goal that could be accomplished within five years is the abolition of institutionally prescribed abuse. Through legislation (and litigation by socially conscious attorneys) we can abolish corporal punishment in public and parochial schools, day care centers, detention homes, foster homes, and other settings where adult caretakers are responsible for children who are not their own. Locally, in every state, and nationally we can enact legislation that will protect children from physical punishment while being cared for by any governmental unit for whatever reason. In many instances, legislation would not be necessary as a first step but as the last. Many schools would probably eliminate corporal punishment if concerned professionals and parents would only question the policy publicly. The elimination of physical violence in privately operated child-caring and child-placing facilities can be effectuated if state authorities will deny license renewals to institutions that abuse and if district attorneys will initiate legal prosecution against them. We know that in many instances social service administrators are unwilling or unable to deny licenses for political or other reasons. Therefore we should insist that the attorney general of the state oversee licensing or at least review licenses when abuse of children is continual, or that the licensing authority be transferred from the state department concerned to the office of the attorney general.

The elimination of physical punishment in private facilities is only the first step in the process. State departments of public welfare must expand their consultation staffs so that, when help is requested or indicated, an employee can be assigned on a temporary basis to assist in the development of alternatives to corporal punishment.

Elimination of corporal punishment in public schools will occur through a reordering of priorities. We must also educate the public as to what we can expect of the schools, and more important, what we cannot. There are probably some older children—in the middle or high schools—whose behavior is held in check by the spectre of the physical force that could be used against them. Special-education personnel and facilities must have priority in meeting the needs of these hard-to-manage children. This would probably require a diversion of funds from such things as athletic programs, a move that might be unpopular with some parents. We must also recognize that when physical punishment is eliminated from the schools there may be some children who will have to be expelled because they cannot adjust to a school setting where violence is not used.

In addition, school boards, parents, teachers, and institutional personnel can and should demand assistance from the schools of education and the departments of psychology at their state universities. Their teacher-training programs should include alternatives to physical punishment and methods of coping with negative behavior and rewarding positive behavior. This assistance from the universities must be practical and down-to-earth, so that it can be applied on an everyday basis. It is obvious that school boards and institutions cannot include quantities of candy in their annual budgets for positive reinforcement. There are much more effective ways of reinforcing desirable behavior, and the universities should lead the way in disseminating this information to persons faced with controlling children every day.

A third short-range goal is the treatment of abuse by the mentally ill and victim-precipitated abuse. These cases should be removed from the agencies currently handling them and referred to community mental health centers, child guidance clinics, or similar mental health agencies with well-trained staff.

Fourth, we must immediately reassess the delivery system and model used for other types of abusers. Our current efforts are haphazard, inefficient, and ineffective. There is a definite need for every state to employ statewide protective service workers who work solely with abuse cases and to whom the usual staffing ratios do not apply. Specialized protective service workers should not carry a caseload of more than 25 adults and their children. With that number of clients the therapist can comfortably see the adults in groups for 90 minutes twice a week and see the children individually. A statewide system is needed so that families in isolated rural areas receive the same type, amount, and quality of service that is given in many urban areas.

As articulated throughout this book, our delivery system must be based on the philosophy that most abusers are not pathological and that treatment must be based on an interpersonal commitment, rather than an ideological model that treats abusers and abused children as inferior.

Intermediate Goals

Our primary intermediate goal must be research, conducted at the national level under the auspices of the cabinet-level agency. One might question why research is recommended as an intermediate goal, rather than as an immediate goal. There are sound reasons for this timing. We must have a basis for a research effort. It is necessary first to determine what we have in the way of programs and where we are going. Then we can launch a serious research effort based on:

1. A theoretical framework suitable to the problem of child abuse.

2. Definition of the questions we wish to ask and the hypotheses we wish to test.

3. Formulation of the data to be gathered and the reasons for gathering them.

4. Formulation of the research design.

5. Evaluation of the data.

Earlier in the book it was mentioned that research is not an activity in which untrained persons or amateurs should be involved. It is a highly technical business that requires extensive preparation, thought, and definition of the problems before data are gathered. To make this a little more understandable, perhaps 60 percent of a trained researcher's efforts go into defining the problem, seeing the need for study, and the theoretical formulations; 38 percent goes into evaluating the data obtained; and only 2 percent of the effort (which is purely mechanical) goes into gathering the data.

This recommendation is made as an alternative to our current "research" effort, which consists of gathering extensive data and then "farming the data." In other words, we are collecting all kinds of meaningless "facts" in child abuse and then using a computer to find out what we have. Computer people have a not very polite expression that is worth remembering, "Garbage in, garbage out." This is but one reason why we need research in the intermediate stage.

During the intermediate stage, we also need to establish a National Parents Institute under the cabinet-level agency and a State Parents Institute in each of the fifty states. The functions of the national institute should be to develop materials that will help parents to be more effective, assist educators and others in finding and using alternative methods of child rearing, and create materials that can be placed in elementary, middle, and high school curriculums. School children should learn about the problems of being a parent and how to cope with those problems. The materials created at the national institute might cover human emotions, various types of social and familial interaction and mechanisms, and sources of help for people in difficulty. The educational package should also teach children at all levels about their bodies and how they function. This information should be taught in a manner that will not be offensive to those who somehow equate knowledge about the heart, liver, spleen, or vagina with immorality.

State parents institutes should serve as vehicles for the dissemination of information to individuals, groups, and organizations and in turn, feed back material and problem areas to the National Parents Institute. While the word *parent* is used in the title, the focus of each institute should be the effect of parental practices on *children*. Each state institute would attempt to identify, record, and follow children who are abused. It should maintain a statewide telephone number that can be called by any person to report child abuse or suspected abuse. The complaint should immediately be forwarded to a local protective service worker for investigation, treatment, and disposition.

Computerized data banks in each state and at the national level should contain the name and any identifying data connected with all abuse and suspected abuse cases. These data banks should be accessible nationwide, twenty-four hours a day for physicians, hospitals, and others who handle abused children so that a child who is transported from one state to another can still be traced. The focus of the data banks must be on the child. There would be legal problems in keeping information on abusers, most certainly if we had a national data bank on suspected abusers. But there can be no objection to keeping track of the child without making any judgments about who abused the child.

Somewhere between the intermediate and long-range goals we need to establish in each community some central resource—perhaps under a state parents institute—where anyone with family problems could go for help: parents experiencing difficulty in child rearing; parents whose children are having problems at school, with playmates, or with siblings; parents whose children are hungry or who have medical problems; and self-identified abusers, who may receive help without stigma. It should operate with the outlook that it is normal to experience problems in child rearing and that it is normal to get exasperated with children's behavior. Similarly, it should seek out and help children who are experiencing difficulties with their parents, and children whose parents reject them or do not understand them should be able to go to the local resource. All may seek advice on what to do, where to go for help, or how to live with an "unlivable" problem. Obviously an agency such as this would not be a child guidance center, a hospital, or any other existing agency. It would combine the efforts of many, and add to them in service.

Long-Range Goals

By the year 2000 we should see the implementation of a Children's Bill of Rights, the extension of the guarantees of the United States Constitution, and an increasing rejection of violence as a means of resolving problems, and any adult who strikes a child or harms one physically will, it is hoped, be considered abusive. At that point, many parents who "spank" only "with the hand" or use a hairbrush or a "switch" will require parental reeducation much the same as the parents of today who are labeled abusers require aid in eliminating certain practices.

The cessation of child abuse implies the end not only of physical damage done to children but of emotional abuse as well. This effort will be time-consuming and difficult but it is one that can be accomplished. The key to our long-range effort to alter the cultural aspects of our society that promulgate and glorify violence done to children will be the clergy and the educators.

After engaging in sophisticated research, we will certainly be in a much better position to know which way we must go. However, it is unlikely that research will challenge one basic goal and belief: Americans must repudiate violence as a method of child rearing. We know many facts about violence, all of which are inimical to good child rearing. We know that physical punishment is one of the least effective means of handling children. While it may result in temporary conformity, it does not bring about any basic changes, and those changes that do occur in children as a result of violence are inevitably negative. Violence does relieve parental anger, but at a terrible cost not only to the child but also to the parent. Violence begets violence, not gentleness or wholesomeness.

As part of our long-range effort, we must carefully and systematically disseminate rational information about violence, its origin, and its effects. We must point out time and time again, until it becomes ingrained in our national character, that violence is negative. Violence stems not from love, but from hate. It proves nothing and resolves nothing. If anything, it only makes a negative situation worse. In child rearing it is a sign of parental weakness not strength. Violence has little relationship to aggression. Aggression is and can be healthy in parents and in all Americans. Unlike violence, it can be warm and beneficial. And likewise, aggression in a child can be very healthy, but violence as a means of resolving problems is most unhealthy.

In the long range, we will probably give some thought to developing alternative roles for children. Currently their roles are few and highly restrictive, the major one in American society being that of student, which has a fairly regimented network of expectations, performance, and activities. Children are now denied entry into the labor force until an advanced age, but this will probably change. Education must accommodate those whose backgrounds are not in tune with the educational establishment. Realistically, there is little or no justification for a nine-month school year. Some children should be in school twelve months a year, some eleven months, and some less. And during the time they are not in school, their education can be continued in a variety of meaningful and productive ways.

We must also work toward the realization that people have the option of choosing whether they wish to have children. Children should be a desired alternative to not having children, rather than the reverse. There is little question that unwanted children are targeted for abuse much more frequently than those whose birth was desired by their parents. The elimination of pressure on couples who do not want children and the availability of birth control information and devices will probably result in a small decrease in child abuse. (And in this respect it would probably be better to revert to the term *birth control* as opposed to *family planning*. The former is honest and implies control, while the latter implies that everyone should have a family but should plan when and why the children will be born.)

Finally, we must make a deliberate effort to change the cultural influences that inculcate children with a feeling of helplessness and hopelessness and with the realization that their very well-being depends on adults. This involves developing a new state of consciousness and an expansion of the role of children. This goal (which also involves deemphasizing Old Testament aspects of child rearing) does not imply a "softening" or "weakening" of our society and its institutions but the maturation of a society that cherishes, protects, and nurtures its members, adult and child alike.

Thus we have come full circle in our study of child abuse, starting and ending in the culture and society in which we live. Child abuse finds its roots in our heritage and is expressed through its members. When we change—and we will change for the better—the problem of child abuse will decline and then disappear.

Today, in many American homes children will be abused. Some will die as the result of physical harm, and an unknown number will be sexually abused. Many will suffer minor harm by being forced to eat soap because of foul language or will be slapped on the face or the buttocks. Some damage will be major, much will be minor. The real question before us is not whether we must change our child-rearing patterns and violence, but how long children must wait before we change.

Appendix
National Standard Form

National Clearinghouse on Child Neglect and Abuse (NCCNA)
P.O. Box 1319, Denver, Colorado 80201

Please use hard ball point pen!

I.D. No. |__|__|__|__|__|__|__|
(1-8)
(NCCNA use only)

1. Name of abused/neglected child(ren):

A _____   C _____
   First   Middle   Last

B _____   D _____

2. Address of child(ren) at time of abuse/neglect: _____
                                      Number   Street

3. Name of parent(s) and/or parent substitute(s) with whom the child(ren) was living at time of abuse/neglect:
        Mother/Substitute   Father/Substitute

_____   _____
First   Middle   Last   First   Middle   Last

4. Name and address of alleged abuser(s)/neglecter(s): _____

5. Worker completing form _____ Date form completed _____

6. _____|_____|_____|_____
(9-19)   City/Town   County   State   District/Region [if applicable]
(NCCNA use only |__|__|__|) (NCCNA use only |__|__|__|) (NCCNA use only |__|__|) (NCCNA use only |__|__|)

7. Community Type: [Mark a (1) in only one space]
(20) ____ Rural   Urban (2500+ population)
              ____ Suburbs
              ____ Inner city
              ____ Not applicable

A. INITIAL REPORT

8. Case number: |__|__|__|__|__|__|__|__|__|__|__|__|__|__|__| (21-35)

9. Source(s) of report: [Mark a (1) in each space that applies] (36-56)

____ Physician (private)   ____ Sibling in the home
____ Physician (hospital)   ____ Sibling out of the home
____ Hospital administrator   ____ Relative in the home
____ Coroner/Medical examiner   ____ Relative out of the home
____ Law enforcement agency   ____ Acquaintance/Neighbor
____ Teacher   ____ Anonymous
____ Court   ____ Unknown
____ Nurse (specify) _____
____ Other School personnel (specify) _____
____ Child-caring agency (specify) _____
____ Public social agency (specify) _____
____ Private social agency (specify) _____
____ Parent/Substitute (specify) _____
____ Other (specify) _____

10. Mandated agency(s) receiving initial report: [Rank order chronologically]
(57-62) ____ State DSS   ____ Court
      ____ County/Local DSS   ____ Law enforcement agency
      ____ Private agency (CPS)   ____ Prosecuting Attorney

11. How report was made to initial mandated receiving agency: [Enter one code only] (63) ____ | 1 By phone   2 In writing   3 In person |

12. Date and Day report received by DSS: (64-70)
Date ____/____/____   Day S M T W Th F S Unk
    mo. day yr.   [Circle one only]

13. Approximate time report received by DSS: (71-75)
____:____ AM/PM [Circle either AM or PM] (99 Unknown)

14. Agency(s) investigating report: [Mark a (1) in each space that applies]
(76-82) ____ State DSS   ____ Court
      ____ County/Local DSS   ____ Law enforcement agency
      ____ Private agency (CPS)   ____ Prosecuting Attorney
      ____ Other (specify) _____

15. Date DSS investigation began: (83-88) ____/____/____
                              mo. day yr.

16. Actions taken by involved agency(s) prior to completion of this form:
[Use agency code numbers provided. Enter code numbers of appropriate agencies.] (89-103)

1	State DSS
2	County/Local DSS
3	Private agency (CPS)
4	Court
5	Law enforcement agency
6	Prosecuting Attorney
7	Other

____ Child temporarily held
____ Emergency removal of child
____ Removal of child court ordered
____ Protective service accepted: child at home
____ Court ordered supervision: child at home
____ Temporary voluntary placement of child
____ Temporary court ordered placement of child
____ Child returned home
____ Consent to adoption
____ Neglect petition: caused to be filed
____ Termination of parental rights
____ Criminal action against the abuser
____ Action awaiting further investigation
____ Report unsubstantiated: no further action contemplated
____ Other (specify) _____

17. Case status: [Mark a (1) in each space that applies]
(104-111) Abuse   Neglect

      ____ Established ____
      ____ Strong indication ____
      ____ Weak indication ____
      ____ Not substantiated ____

IF UNSUBSTANTIATED, DO NOT COMPLETE REST OF FORM!

18. Further action planned by DSS: [Mark a (1) in each space that applies]
(112-133)____ Child protective services
____ Neglect petition to be filed
____ Court ordered supervision child at home
____ Temporary court ordered placement of child
____ Temporary voluntary placement of child
____ Child to be returned to the home
____ Initiate termination of parental rights
____ Recommend criminal action
____ Day care services   ____ Family planning
____ Homemaker services   ____ Marital counseling
____ Public assistance   ____ Foster care
____ Family counseling   ____ Unknown
____ Other child welfare services   ____ None
    (specify)_____
____ Outpatient mental health treatment
    (for whom) _____

_____ Inpatient mental health treatment
(for whom) _____
_____ Other health services
_____ Other (specify) _____

B. CHILDREN

19. Date of birth and sex of children.
Child(ren) Involved in abuse/neglect:

	Date of birth mo. day yr.	Sex	1 Male	2 Female	9 Unknown	
A	___/___/___	____				(134-140)
B	___/___/___	____				(141-147)
C	___/___/___	____				(148-154)
D	___/___/___	____				(155-161)

Other child(ren) in family:

E	___/___/___	____	(162-168)
F	___/___/___	____	(169-175)
G	___/___/___	____	(176-182)
H	___/___/___	____	(183-189)

20. Status of child(ren): *[Enter only one code per child]* (190-197)

Child(ren) involved				Other Child(ren)
A ___	1 Legitimate	4 Foster		E ___
B ___	2 Illegitimate	5 Other		F ___
C ___	3 Adopted	9 Unknown		G ___
D ___				H ___

21. Parent-child relationship *[Enter only one code per child]* (9-16)

Child(ren) involved			Other Child(ren)
A ___	1 Mother and Father		E ___
B ___	2 Mother only	5 Foster	F ___
C ___	3 Father only	6 Other	G ___
D ___	4 Adopted	9 Unknown	H ___

22. Special characteristics of the child(ren): *[Mark a (1) in each space that applies, a (0) in each space that does not apply, and a (9) for unknown]*

Child(ren) Involved A B C D		Other Child(ren) E F G H	
☐☐☐☐	Premature	☐☐☐☐	(17-24)
☐☐☐☐	Mentally retarded	☐☐☐☐	(25-32)
☐☐☐☐	Physically handicapped	☐☐☐☐	(33-40)
☐☐☐☐	Chronic Illness	☐☐☐☐	(41-48)
☐☐☐☐	Product of multiple birth	☐☐☐☐	(49-56)
☐☐☐☐	Congenital handicap	☐☐☐☐	(57-64)
☐☐☐☐	Emotionally disturbed	☐☐☐☐	(65-72)
☐☐☐☐	No special characteristics	☐☐☐☐	(73-80)
☐☐☐☐	Unknown	☐☐☐☐	(81-88)
☐☐☐☐	Other (specify) _____	☐☐☐☐	(89-96)

23. Current grade level of child(ren): *[Enter one code per child]* (97-112)

Child(ren) Involved			Other Child(ren)
A ___	00 Not yet enrolled	13 Other	E ___
B ___	P Preschool	14 Withdrawn	F ___
C ___	01-12 Enter grade level	99 Unknown	G ___
D ___			H ___

24. Ethnicity/Citizenship of child(ren): *[Mark a (1) in each space that applies]*

Child(ren) Involved A B C D		Other Child(ren) E F G H	
☐☐☐☐	Caucasian	☐☐☐☐	(113-120)
☐☐☐☐	Black	☐☐☐☐	(121-128)
☐☐☐☐	Spanish surname	☐☐☐☐	(129-136)
☐☐☐☐	American Indian	☐☐☐☐	(137-144)
☐☐☐☐	Asian (specify)	☐☐☐☐	(145-152)
☐☐☐☐	Alien parentage	☐☐☐☐	(153-160)
☐☐☐☐	Other (specify)	☐☐☐☐	(161-168)
☐☐☐☐	Unknown	☐☐☐☐	(169-176)

25. Previous record/evidence of abuse/neglect: *[Enter only one code per child]* (177-184)

Child(ren) Involved			Other Child(ren)
A ___	0 None	4 Evidence of neglect	E ___
B ___	1 Record of abuse	5 Record of abuse and neglect	F ___
C ___	2 Evidence of abuse	6 Evidence of abuse-neglect	G ___
D ___	3 Record of neglect	9 Unknown	H ___

C. HOUSEHOLD *[Where child(ren) resided at the time of abuse/neglect]*

26. Adult household member(s): *[Enter the number of individuals in each category in the appropriate space]* (9-26)

M	F		M	F	
___	___	Natural parent	___	___	Grandparent
___	___	Adoptive parent	___	___	Other relative
___	___	Stepparent	___	___	No relationship
___	___	Foster parent	___	___	Relationship unknown
___	___	Paramour			

27. Approximate ages of parent(s)/substitute(s): (27-30)
_____ Mother/sub.   _____ Father/sub.   (99 Unknown)

28. Marital status of parent(s)/substitute(s): *[Enter one item only]* (31)

_____	1 Legal marriage	5 Widow/widower
	2 Consensual union	6 Marriage partner temporarily absent
	3 Never married	7 Marriage partner permanently absent
	4 Divorced/separated	9 Unknown

29. Ethnicity/Citizenship of parent(s)/substitute(s): *[Mark a (1) in each space that applies]* (32-47)

Mo.	Fa.		Mo.	Fa.		Mo.	Fa.	
___	___	Caucasian	___	___	American Indian	___	___	Alien
___	___	Black	___	___	Spanish surname	___	___	Unknown
___	___	Asian (specify)						
___	___	Other (specify) _____						

30. Religion of parent(s)/sub.(s): *[Enter only one code per parent]* (48-49)

Mo. ___	1 Protestant	4 Other (specify) _____
Fa. ___	2 Catholic	5 None
	3 Jewish	9 Unknown

31. Education of parent(s)/sub.(s): *[Enter only one code per parent]* (50-51)

	0 No education	5 Some college/Vocational training
Mo. ___	1 Grades 1 - 3	6 College graduate
	2 Grades 4 - 6	7 Post graduate
Fa. ___	3 Grades 7 - 9	9 Unknown
	4 Grades 10 - 12	

32. Occupation of parent(s)/substitute(s):
Mo. _____ (NCCNA use only ☐☐☐) (52-54)
Fa. _____ (NCCNA use only ☐☐☐) (55-57)

33. Estimated yearly family gross income:

From employment	$ ☐☐☐☐☐	(58-62)
From public assistance	$ ☐☐☐☐☐	(63-67)
From other sources	$ ☐☐☐☐☐	(68-72)
Total	$ ☐☐☐☐☐	(73-77)

34. Agency(s) active within two years prior to the occurrence: *[Mark a (1) in each space that applies]* (78-83)
_____ Private Agency   _____ Public Agency   _____ Court
_____ Unknown   _____ None (If none or unknown skip No. 35)
_____ Other (specify) _____

35. Type of services provided by above agency(s): *[Mark a (1) in each space that applies]* (84-97)

_____ Child protective services	_____ Family planning
_____ Day care services	_____ Marital counseling
_____ Homemaker services	_____ Foster care
_____ Public assistance	_____ Unknown
_____ Family counseling	

___ Other child welfare services (specify) _____
___ Outpatient mental health treatment (for whom)_____
___ Inpatient mental health treatment (for whom) _____
___ Other health services
___ Other (specify) _____

36. Type of housing: *[Enter one code only]* (98)

| _____ | 1 Public | 2 Private | 9 Unknown |

37. Number of rooms in dwelling: (99-101)
_____ Total rooms (99 Unknown)   _____ Rooms for sleeping (9 Unknown)

38. Assessment of sleeping facilities: *[Mark a (1) in each space that applies]* (102)
___ Adequate   Inadequate
              ___ Overcrowded
              ___ Mixture of adults and children
              ___ Mixture of adolescent siblings of opposite sex
              ___ Other (specify) _____
___ Unknown

39. Assessment of housing conditions: *[Enter one code only]* (103)

_____	1 Substandard	4 Above average
	2 Dilapidated	9 Unknown
	3 Adequate	

D. FACTS OF ALLEGED ABUSE/NEGLECT

40. Date and day of abuse incident: (104-110)

Date ___/___/___ Day S M T W Th F S Unk
     mo.   day   yr.   *[Circle one code only]*

41. Approx. time of abuse incident: _____ : _____ AM/PM *[Circle either AM or PM]* (111-115) (99 Unknown)

42. Place of occurrence of abuse/neglect: *[Enter one code only]* (116)

_____	1 Child's household	6 Treatment facility
	2 Other private household	7 Correctional institution
	3 Day care center	8 Other (specify)
	4 Day school	_____
	5 Boarding school	9 Unknown

43. Type of abuse/neglect *[Mark a (1) in each space that applies]*
Child(ren)
A B C D
⊔⊔⊔⊔ No visible injuries (117-120)
⊔⊔⊔⊔ Contusions (121-124)
⊔⊔⊔⊔ Abrasions (125-128)
⊔⊔⊔⊔ Lacerations (129-132)
⊔⊔⊔⊔ Sprains, dislocations (133-136)
⊔⊔⊔⊔ Internal injuries (137-140)
⊔⊔⊔⊔ Exploitation (141-144)
⊔⊔⊔⊔ Malnutrition (145-148)
⊔⊔⊔⊔ Exposure to elements (149-152)
⊔⊔⊔⊔ Burns, scalding (153-156)
⊔⊔⊔⊔ Bone fracture (other than skull) (157-160)
⊔⊔⊔⊔ Skull fracture (161-164)
⊔⊔⊔⊔ Subdural hemorrhage or hematoma (165-168)
⊔⊔⊔⊔ Dismemberment (169-172)
⊔⊔⊔⊔ Brain damage (173-176)
⊔⊔⊔⊔ Poisoning (177-180)
⊔⊔⊔⊔ Congenital drug addition (181-184)
⊔⊔⊔⊔ Environmental drug addiction (185-188)
⊔⊔⊔⊔ Failure to thrive (189-192)
⊔⊔⊔⊔ Physical neglect (193-196)
⊔⊔⊔⊔ Emotional neglect (197-200)
⊔⊔⊔⊔ Medical neglect (9-12)
⊔⊔⊔⊔ Moral neglect (13-16)
⊔⊔⊔⊔ Educational neglect (17-20)

⊔⊔⊔⊔ Abandonment (21-24)
⊔⊔⊔⊔ Unknown (25-28)
⊔⊔⊔⊔ Sexual abuse (specify)_____ (29-32)
⊔⊔⊔⊔ Other (specify) _____ (33-36)

44. Manner in which physical abuse was inflicted: *[Mark a (1) in each space that applies]*
Child(ren)
A B C D
⊔⊔⊔⊔ Beating with hands (37-40)
⊔⊔⊔⊔ Beating with instruments (41-44)
⊔⊔⊔⊔ Kicking (45-48)
⊔⊔⊔⊔ Biting (49-52)
⊔⊔⊔⊔ Strangling or suffocating (53-56)
⊔⊔⊔⊔ Drowning (57-60)
⊔⊔⊔⊔ Shooting (61-64)
⊔⊔⊔⊔ Stabbing (65-68)
⊔⊔⊔⊔ Burning or scalding (69-72)
⊔⊔⊔⊔ Poisoning (73-76)
⊔⊔⊔⊔ Locking in or tying (77-80)
⊔⊔⊔⊔ Locking out (81-84)
⊔⊔⊔⊔ Unknown (85-88)
⊔⊔⊔⊔ Other (specify) _____ (89-92)

45. Describe neglect conditions: _____
_____
_____
_____

46. Severity of injuries resulting from abuse/neglect: *[Mark a (1) in each space that applies]*
Child(ren)
A B C D
⊔⊔⊔⊔ No medical treatment required/child seen by physician (93-96)
⊔⊔⊔⊔ Appeared not to require medical treatment/child not seen by physician (97-100)
⊔⊔⊔⊔ Appeared to require medical treatment/treatment not sought (101-104)
⊔⊔⊔⊔ Received outpatient medical treatment (105-108)
⊔⊔⊔⊔ Received hospitalization for medical treatment (109-112)
⊔⊔⊔⊔ No psychiatric treatment required/child seen by physician (113-116)
⊔⊔⊔⊔ Appeared not to require psychiatric treatment/child not seen by physician (117-120)
⊔⊔⊔⊔ Appeared to require psychiatric treatment/treatment not sought (121-124)
⊔⊔⊔⊔ Received outpatient psychiatric treatment (125-128)
⊔⊔⊔⊔ Hospitalized for psychiatric treatment (129-132)
⊔⊔⊔⊔ Dead on arrival (133-136)
⊔⊔⊔⊔ Death, not immediate (137-140)
⊔⊔⊔⊔ Unknown (141-144)

E. PERSON(S) ALLEGEDLY RESPONSIBLE FOR ABUSE/NEGLECT

If incident occurred in an institution, complete all appropriate items.

47. Identity of alleged abuser(s)/neglecter(s): *[Enter one code only]* (145)

| _____ | 1 Known | 2 Suspected | 9 Unknown |

48. Relationship to child(ren) involved in abuse/neglect: *[Enter one code only per child]* (146-161)

	Ab/Neg I	Ab/Neg II	01 Natural parent	07 Relative
A	_____	_____	02 Adoptive parent	08 Babysitter
B	_____	_____	03 Stepparent	09 Staff of institution
C	_____	_____	04 Foster parent	10 Teacher
D	_____	_____	05 Sibling	11 Other (specify)
			06 Parent's paramour	99 Unknown

49. Age of alleged abuser(s)/neglecter(s):-(162-165) I _____ II _____

50. Sex of alleged abuser(s)/neglecter(s): *[Enter one code only per person]* (166-167) I _____ II _____ | 1 Male | 2 Female | 9 Unknown |

51. Ethnicity/Citizenship of alleged abuser(s)/neglecter(s): *[Mark a (1) in each space that applies]* (168-183)

Ab/Neg I	Ab/Neg II		Ab/Neg I	Ab/Neg II	
_____	_____	Caucasian	_____	_____	American Indian
_____	_____	Black	_____	_____	Alien
_____	_____	Spanish surname	_____	_____	Unknown
_____	_____	Asian (specify) _____			
_____	_____	Other (specify) _____			

52. Does alleged abuser(s)/neglecter(s) live in home of abused/neglected child(ren): *[Enter one code only per abuser/neglecter]* (184-185)

Ab/Neg I   II

| 0 No | 1 Yes | 9 Unknown |

53. Does alleged abuser(s)/neglecter(s) have a known record of having abused/ neglected previously: *[Enter one code only per abuser/neglecter]* (186-187)

Ab/Neg I   II

0 No	3 Yes, abuse and neglect
1 Yes, abuse	9 Unknown
2 Yes, neglect	

54. Stress factors immediately prior to abuse incident: *[Mark a (1) in each space that applies, a (0) in each that does not and a (9) for unknown]* (9-34)

Ab/Neg I	Ab/Neg II	
_____	_____	Family break up
_____	_____	Job related difficulties
_____	_____	Health problem
_____	_____	Argument
_____	_____	Physical fight
_____	_____	Under the influence of alcohol
_____	_____	Other drug (specify) _____
_____	_____	Child's incessant crying
_____	_____	Child's disobedience/loss of control during discipline
_____	_____	Child's hostility or provocation
_____	_____	Child's resistance to perpetrator's sexual advances
_____	_____	Other immediate stress: (specify) _____
_____	_____	None apparent

55. Assessment of ongoing stress affecting alleged abuser(s)/neglecter(s): *[Mark a (1) in each space that applies, a (0) in each that does not, and a (9) for unknown]* (35-88)

Ab/Neg I	Ab/Neg II	
_____	_____	Insufficent income
_____	_____	Heavy financial debt
_____	_____	Misuse of adequate income
_____	_____	Unemployment
_____	_____	Poor work stability
_____	_____	Physical illness or injury
_____	_____	Alcohol addiction
_____	_____	Other drug addiction
_____	_____	Mental retardation
_____	_____	Recent discharge from mental health facility
_____	_____	Currently receiving treatment at mental health facility
_____	_____	Marital
_____	_____	Religious differences
_____	_____	Work related
_____	_____	New baby in home
_____	_____	Pregnancy
_____	_____	Heavy continuous child care responsibility
_____	_____	Absence of essential family member
_____	_____	Physical abuse of spouse
_____	_____	Police/court record (excluding traffic)
_____	_____	Newcomer to household
_____	_____	Recent relocation
_____	_____	History of abuse as a child
_____	_____	Repetition of family style
_____	_____	Normal method of discipline; self-definition of abuser/ neglecter as stern, authoritarian, disciplinarian
_____	_____	Other (specify) _____
_____	_____	None apparent

COMMENTS:

National Standard Form — 0023
©Copyright 1974, Children's Division, The American Humane Association, Denver, Colo.

Bibliography

Arnold v. *Carpenter,* 459 F.2d 939 (1972).

Asch, Stuart S. 1968. "Crib Deaths: Their Possible Relationship to Post-Partum Depression and Infanticide." *Journal of Mount Sinai Hospital* (New York) 35: 214–20.

Bakan, David. 1971. *Slaughter of the Innocents: A Study of the Battered Child Phenomenon.* San Francisco: Jossey-Bass.

Baron, Michael A.; Bejar, Rafael L.; and Sheaff, Peter J. 1970. "Neurologic Manifestations of the Battered Child Syndrome." *Pediatrics* 45: 1003–1007.

Bennie, E. H., and Sclare, A. S. 1969. "The Battered Child Syndrome." *American Journal of Psychiatry* 125: 975–79.

Biermann, G. 1969. *Kindeszuchtigung und Kindesmisshandlung.* ("Chastisement and Mistreatment of Children"). Munich: Ernst Reinhard.

Birrell, R. G., and Birrell, J. H. W. 1968. "The Maltreatment Syndrome in Children: A Hospital Survey." *Medical Journal of Australia* 55–2: 1023–29.

Brown, John A., and Daniels, Robert. 1968. "Some Observations on Abusive Parents." *Child Welfare* 47: 89–94.

Caffey, John; Silverman, Frederick N.; Kempe, C. Henry; Venters, Homer; and Leonard, Martha. 1972. "Child Battery: Seek and Save." *Medical World News* 12: 21, 25, 28, 32–33.

Cameron, J. Malcolm. 1972. "The Battered Baby." *Nursing Mirror and Midwives Journal* 134: 32–38.

Clinard, Marshall, and Quinney, Richard. 1967. *Criminal Behavior Systems: A Typology.* New York: Holt, Rinehart & Winston.

Curtis, George C. 1963. "Violence Breeds Violence—Perhaps?" *American Journal of Psychiatry* 120: 386–87.

D'Ambrosio, Richard. 1970. "Treatment of a Battered Child." In *No Language But a Cry,* Garden City, N.Y.: Doubleday.

DeFrancis, Vincent. 1971. *Termination of Parental Rights: Balancing the Equities.* Denver: American Humane Association (Children's Division).

Ebbin, Allan; Gollub, Michael H.; Stein, Arthur M.; and Wilson, Miriam G. 1969. "Battered Child Syndrome at the Los Angeles County General Hospital." *American Journal of Diseases of Children* 118: 660–67.

Elmer, Elizabeth. 1966. "Hazards in Determining Child Abuse." *Child Welfare* 45: 28–33.

————. 1967. "Child Abuse: The Family's Cry for Help." *Journal of Psychiatric Nursing* 5: 332–41.

————, and Gregg, Grace S. 1967. "Developmental Characteristics of Abused Children." *Pediatrics* 40: 596–602.

Evans, Sue L.; Reinhart, John B.; and Succop, Ruth A. 1972. "Failure to Thrive: A Study of 45 Children and Their Families." *Journal of the American Academy of Child Psychiatry* 11: 440–57.

Fleming, G. M. 1967. "Cruelty to Children." *British Medical Journal* 5549: 421–22.

Flynn, William R. 1970. "Frontier Justice: A Contribution to the Theory of Child Battery." *American Journal of Psychiatry* 127: 375–79.

Fontana, Vincent J. 1971a. *The Maltreated Child.* 2d ed. Springfield, Ill.: Charles C. Thomas.

————. 1971b. "Which Parents Abuse Children?" *Medical Insight* 3: 16–21.

Galdston, Richard. 1971. "Violence Begins at Home: The Parents' Center Project for the Study and Prevention of Child Abuse." *Journal of the American Academy of Child Psychiatry* 10: 226–50.

Gil, David. 1973. *Violence against Children.* Cambridge: Harvard University Press.

Groezinger, Jean. 1974. "Interview Schedule in Sexual Abuse of Children." Unpublished. Department of Forensic Studies, Indiana University, Bloomington.

Havens, Leton L. 1972. "Youth, Violence, and the Nature of Family Life." *Psychiatric Annals* 2: 18–21, 23–25, 29.

Heins, Marilyn. 1969. "Child Abuse: Analysis of a Current Epidemic." *Michigan Medicine* 68: 887–91.

Holter, Joan C., and Friedman, Stanford B. 1968. "Principles of Management in Child Abuse Cases." *American Journal of Orthopsychiatry* 38: 127–36.

James, Joseph, Jr. 1972. "Child Neglect and Abuse." *Maryland State Medical Journal* 21: 64–65.

Jeffress, Elizabeth. 1967. "Psychological Aspects of Pediatric Practice." *Journal of the American Women's Association* 22: 630–33.

Karpman, Benjamin. 1954. *The Sexual Offender and His Offenses.* New York: Julian Press.

Kempe, C. Henry. 1971. "Paediatric Implications of the Battered Baby Syndrome." *Archives of Disease in Childhood* 46: 28–37.

———, and Helfer, Ray E. 1972. *Helping the Battered Child and His Family*. Philadelphia: J. B. Lippincott.

Laury, Gabriel V. 1970. "The Battered Child Syndrome: Parental Motivation, Clinical Aspects." *Bulletin of the New York Academy of Medicine* 46: 676–85.

McClung, Merle. 1974. "The Right to Learn." *Trial* 10 (May/June): 27.

McKinney, John C. 1966. *Constructive Typology and Social Theory*. New York: Appleton-Century-Crofts.

Martignoni, Margaret, ed. 1955. *The Illustrated Treasury of Children's Literature*. New York: Grosset and Dunlap.

Michael, Marianne K. 1970. "The Battered Child." *Iowa Journal of Social Work* 3: 78–83.

National Standard Form. 1974. Denver: American Humane Association (Children's Division).

Nau, E., and Cabanis, D. 1966. "Kaspar Hauser Syndrome." *Munchener Medizinische Wochenschrift* 108: 929–31.

Paulson, Morris J., and Blake, Phillip R. 1969. "The Physically Abused Child: A Focus on Prevention." *Child Welfare* 48: 86–95.

Pavenstedt, Eleanor, and Bernard, Viola. 1971. *Crises of Family Disorganization: Programs to Soften Their Impact on Children*. New York: Behavioral Publications.

Pawlikowski, Andrzej. 1972. "Losy Dzieci z Rodzin Alkoholikow" ("Fates of Children from Families of Alcoholics"). *Problemy Alkoholizmu* (Warsaw) 7: 4–6.

Pickel, Stuart; Anderson, Charles; and Holiday, Malcolm A. 1970. "Thirsting and Hypernatremic Dehydration: A Form of Child Abuse." *Pediatrics* 45: 54–59.

Pospisil-Zavrski, K., and Turcin, R. 1968. "Alkoholizam I Cl. 196. KZ —Zlostavljanje I Zapustanse" ("Alcoholism and the 196th Article of the Yugoslavian Penal Code: Mistreatment and Neglect of Juveniles"). *Neurophsihijatrija* (Zagreb) 16: 49–53.

Reichel-Dolmatoff, Gerado. 1951. *Los Kogi: A Tribe of the Sierra Nevada of Santa Marta, Colombia*. Bogota: Editorial Iqueima.

Richette, Lisa. 1969. *The Throwaway Children*. Philadelphia: J. B. Lippincott.

Rosen, Shirley; Hirschenfang, Samuel; and Benton, Joseph G. 1967. "Aftermath of Severe Multiple Deprivation in a Young Child: Clinical Implications." *Perceptual and Motor Skills* 24: 219–26.

Sattin, Dana B., and Millet, John K. 1971. "The Ecology of Child Abuse within a Military Community." *American Journal of Orthopsychiatry* 41: 675–78.

Silver, Larry B.; Dublin, Christia; and Lourie, Reginald S. 1971. "Agency Action and Interaction in Cases of Child Abuse." *Social Casework* 52: 164–71.

Skinner, A. E., and Castle, R. L. 1969. *Seventy-Eight Battered Children: A Retrospective Study.* Hoddeston, Herts., England: Thomas Knight.

Spinetta, John J., and Rigler, David. 1972. "The Child-Abusing Parent: A Psychological Review." *Psychological Bulletin* 77: 296–304.

Steele, Brand F., and Pollack, Carl C. 1968. "A Psychiatric Study of Parents Who Abuse Infants and Small Children." In Helfer, R., ed., *The Battered Child,* Chicago: University of Chicago Press.

Stoenner, Herb. 1973. *Plain Talk about Child Abuse.* Denver: *The Denver Post,* 1972. Reprinted by the American Humane Association, Denver.

Straus, P., and Wolf, A. 1969. "Un Sujet d'actualité: les enfants maltraites" ("A Topical Subject: The Battered Child"). *Psychiatrie de l'Enfant* (Paris) 12: 577–628.

Swanson, David M. 1968. "Adult Sexual Abuse of Children." *Diseases of the Nervous System* 29: 677–83.

Terr, Lenore C. 1970. "A Family Study of Child Abuse." *American Journal of Psychiatry* 127: 665–71.

————, and Watson, Andrew S. 1968. "The Battered Child Rebrutalized: 10 Cases of Medical-Legal Confusion." *American Journal of Psychiatry* 124: 1432–39.

Toussaint, M. 1971. "La Societé et l'enfant victime de mauvais traitement" ("Society and the Child Victim of Cruel Treatment"). *Les Enfants victimes de mauvais traitements* (Brussels) 28: 83–88.

Wertham, Frederic. 1972. "Battered Children and Baffled Adults." *Bulletin of the New York Academy of Medicine* 48: 887–98.

Weston, James T. 1968. "The Pathology in Child Abuse." In Helfer, R., ed., *The Battered Child,* Chicago: University of Chicago Press.

Wisconsin v. *Yoder,* 406 U.S. 205 (1972).

Wolfgang, Marvin, and Ferracuti, Franco. 1967. *Subculture of Violence: Towards an Integrated Theory of Criminology.* London: Tavistock.

Wright, Logan. 1970. "Psychological Aspects of the Battered Child Syndrome. *Southern Medical Bulletin* 58: 14–18.

Young, Leontine. 1964. *Wednesday's Children.* New York: McGraw-Hill.

Zalba, S. R. 1966. "The Abused Child: I. A Survey of the Problem." *Social Work* 11: 8.

Zuckerman, Kenneth; Ambuel, J. Philip; and Sandman, Rosalyn. 1972. "Child Neglect and Abuse: A Study of Cases Evaluated at Columbus Children's Hospital in 1968–1969." *Ohio State Medical Journal* 68: 629–32.

Index

Abused children, traits of: guilt feelings, 157; physical underdevelopment, 158–159; speech defects, 158–159; untruthfulness, 162
Accidental or unknowing abuser, 44–45, 103–104
Alternative coping mechanisms, 87–89
American Journal of Roentgenology, 20
Arnold v. *Carpenter*, 109

Battered child syndrome, 20
Behavior, irritating, 86–87
Bible: child rearing and, 9, 10–12, 16–17, 48–49, 180; sexual abuse and, 115

Caffey, John, 20
Causes of abuse: alcohol, 21; Bible, 10–12; cultural heritage, 22; emotional pressures, 21–22; family stress, 21; guilt, 85; historical, 9–10; inadequate laws, 71; learned behavior, 23; literary, 12–16; neglect, 21, 28–29, 102–103; "organic inferiority," 21; "organic neural overload," 21; organicity, 21; parental mental retardation, 21; pathological view, 23; poverty, 21, 22–23, 36; psychosis and neurosis, 22; traits of abusers, 22
Child prostitution, 129
Child rearing: Bible and, 9, 48, 180; cessation of physical punishment, 178; confidential areas, 66; cultural heritage, 170; discipline, 33, 39; learned behavior, 23, 37–39; philosophy of, 7, 71–72, 94, 178; qual-

ity of interaction, 94; replication of parental practice, 37–39; rights of children and, 71–72; strategies for change, 170–172; toilet training, 86; violence in, 178–179; young parents, 39
Children's Bill of Rights, 178
Clinical tradeoff, 101
Confidential areas, 66
Coping mechanisms, 85, 87–89
Crying by abusive females, 76
Cultural heritage: need for change, 180; sex "education," 131–132; socially and parentally incompetent abuser and, 97–98; subcultural abuser and, 105–106

Defining abuse: cultural differences, 25–26; emotional, 36–37; emphasis on child, 27–28; legal, 33–34; misuse of label, 42; neglect, 28; physical, 27–28; prejudices and biases, 33; problems of, 24–29, 34; restrictions of, 28–29; sexual, 26, 29; theory construction, 32; traditional, 6–7
Denial of abuse, 76
Determination of abuse, 58–60
Discipline: cessation of physical punishment, 178; in institutions, 108–110; reinforcement of negative behavior, 47; spanking, 5, 51
Displacement, 39–40

Family triad, 82–84, 121–126
Foster care: evaluation of, 67–68; initial contact, 160–161; mentally ill parents and, 107

189